ROAR OF THE ROAD
The Story of Auto Racing

BOOKS BY HAL BUTLER

Baseball All Star Game Thrills
The Bob Allison Story
The Harmon Killebrew Story
Roar of the Road
The Story of Auto Racing
Stormin' Norman Cash
There's Nothing New in Sports
The Story of How Sports Began

HAL BUTLER

ROAR OF THE ROAD

The Story of Auto Racing

Photographs

JULIAN MESSNER  NEW YORK

Published simultaneously in the United States and Canada by Julian Messner, a division of Simon & Schuster, Inc., 1 West 39 Street, New York, N.Y. 10018. All rights reserved.

Picture research Alice Marti

Printed in the United States of America
SBN 671–32119–6 Cloth trade
671–32120–0 MCE
Library of Congress Catalog Card No. 69–12108

INTRODUCTION

This is not the story of automobiles, as such—how they were born or how they are manufactured. This is the story of how they are raced.

It has often been said that automobile racing is a form of madness, and there is some truth to the statement. Among the most daring, and sometimes most reckless, men of our time are the automobile race drivers. Each year they risk their lives in such torrid competition as the famed Indianapolis 500, stock car races all across the country and sports car races at Le Mans and Sebring and other well-known circuits, as well as in such fantastic tests of endurance, skill and raw courage as Grand Prix racing in almost every country conscious of the automobile.

This is the story of how automobile racing began, and what it has become. For the convenience of the reader, it is divided into sections. It covers the first feeble attempts at racing the early contraptions known as "horseless carriages," traces the development of Grand Prix racing and sports car events, tells the story of oval track racing and, as a final touch, discusses drag racing, rallies, ghymkanas, hill climbs and other competitive events.

If you are a car buff—a lover of automobiles—this book is for you.

CONTENTS

PART ONE The Early Races

Chapter   1   The World's First
              Automobile Race
          2   The Town-to-Town Races
          3   Peking to Paris
          4   New York to Paris
          5   The Gordon Bennett Races
          6   The Vanderbilt Cup Races

PART TWO The Grand Prix Circuit

Chapter   1   The French Grand Prix
              (Mike Hawthorn)
          2   The Monaco Grand Prix
              (Jack Brabham)

3   The German Grand Prix
(Juan Manuel Fangio)
4   The Grand Prix of Holland
(Joakim Bonnier)
5   The Belgian Grand Prix
(Tony Brooks)
6   The Italian Grand Prix
(Juan Manuel Fangio)
7   The British Grand Prix
(Froilan Gonzalez)

PART THREE   The Sports Car Circuit

Chapter 1   The Twenty-Four Hours of Le Mans
(Pierre Levegh, Dan Gurney, A. J. Foyt)
2   Italy's Unbelievable Mille Miglia
(Stirling Moss)
3   The Targa Florio
(Achille Varzi)
4   The Twelve Hours of Sebring
(Mario Andretti, Bruce McLaren)

PART FOUR   Oval Track Racing

Chapter 1   The Indianapolis 500
(Ray Harroun, Bill Vukovich, Jim Clark)

PART FIVE   The Stocks, the Midgets and Other Things

Chapter 1   Stock Cars and Midgets
2   The Sports Car Phenomenon
3   The Lure of the Drag Strip

Postscript
Index

PART ONE

THE EARLY RACES

THE WORLD'S FIRST 1
AUTOMOBILE RACE

It was June 22, 1894, in Paris, France. The Marquis de Dion sat on the high seat of the ugly automobile he had built and shivered nervously at what was to come. The car was called a De Dion Bouton—eventually to become one of the best-known of the world's early automobiles—but today it was only a fiery contraption that frightened horses and people and sometimes even the man who had created it.

Today, too, this fantastic "horseless carriage" was

to take part in the first automobile race of all time. To the Marquis de Dion, this was indeed the most frightening aspect of all.

Since the early 1890s the French had been pioneering in the business of building automobiles and were already turning out what was then a sizable production of cars. But the idea of racing them was a new development. It had occurred because each automobile manufacturer was anxious to demonstrate to the French public that *his* car was the best. And in what better way could a car-maker do this than to win a race that would prove the superiority of his own car?

So it was that in the summer of 1894 the leaders of the budding French automobile industry got together and planned a race called the *Course de Voitures sans Chevaux*—race of the horseless carriages. It was to be run between Paris and Rouen, an incredible distance of 78 miles, and no one—not even the manufacturers—was certain that any of the cars in the race could make the distance.

The French people, as a whole, were unconcerned about the affair. Automobiles were playthings of the wealthy and had not as yet made sufficient impression on the French mind for the average citizen to pay much attention to the event. It sounded to them like a foolish idea dreamed up by fanatics who had nothing better to do.

But to the Marquis de Dion and his car-making opponents, Paris-to-Rouen was the big event of the year.

The Marquis, perched birdlike on his high seat, looked down at his mechanic as the greasy little man clambered over the car.

"Is she set to go?" he asked anxiously.

"As good as she'll ever be," said the mechanic.

The Marquis nodded. "Full steam ahead, then," he said with satisfaction.

The word "steam" was most accurate. The De Dion Bouton was a steam-driven car, fired by coal. It was being challenged by twenty other French cars, many propelled by "liquid fuel"—gasoline. Among them were the Peugeot and the Panhard, both to become famous French makes in later years.

The grotesque cars lumbered to the starting line, their engines—most of them boasting only two or three horsepower—alternately roaring, sputtering and stalling as anxious mechanics tinkered to keep them alive. This Paris-to-Rouen contest was not, in today's sense, a race of speed. True, cars would compete on the basis of elapsed time between Paris and Rouen, but mostly it was a contest of endurance. No one knew how long the cars would hold up over the 78-mile course. No one was even sure if any of the cars could complete the unbelievable test of endurance. It was conceded that the toughest car, with the best mechanic and the most luck, would win the automotive world's first race.

When the 21 competing vehicles—all big, bulky, misshapen monsters—were finally lined up, a signal was given and the big race was under way. The Marquis felt his huge car lurch beneath him. Right behind came the other cars, their engines roaring and whining. Within a few minutes the chugging cars were beyond the Paris city limits and were bumping over a rutted unpaved road.

The Marquis clutched the tiller, guiding the car down the center of the road by sheer strength. Every time the car hit a bump with its hard, solid tires, it veered toward the ditches on either side of the road, and de Dion would force the car back on the road again. Meanwhile, his agile mechanic refused to remain in his seat. Instead he climbed all over the car, tinkering with this, checking on that.

"Keep her going!" he shouted. "Leave it to me to keep it from falling apart!"

The mechanic literally did just that. With wrenches in hand, he tightened bolts and nuts as the car traveled, making sure that the big rattletrap didn't lose a vital part in the middle of the road.

The De Dion Bouton had taken the lead, with the gasoline-engine cars close behind. The drivers of the gasoline-powered cars had a hazard to face that they had not counted on. The De Dion Bouton, steam-driven, was disgorging fiery chunks of coal as it ran, scattering glowing embers along the road. The opposing drivers were gasping. It was a big enough adventure just to drive a car in this mad race, without having to drive it through a shower of fire!

French farmers came to the fences surrounding their land and watched the strange parade go by. Many of them had never before seen an automobile, and the fiery discharge from the De Dion Bouton and the frightful noise of the other cars dismayed them. In anger, they shook their fists at the drivers.

"Firebugs!" they screamed.

"Insane fools!"

"Maniacs!"

"*Mon Dieu,* you will set the world on fire with your foolishness!"

But the race went on. And as it progressed, mechanical trouble became a major factor. Cars broke down. Engines stalled. Mechanics frantically got the cars going again, only to have them break down later—for some other reason. The farther the cars traveled, the more stalling occurred. Several of the cars stopped and refused to budge again, thus eliminating their disappointed drivers from the race. Others were nursed along, mile after slow mile, their drivers and mechanics determined to make the distance to Rouen even if they had to push the vehicle over the finish line.

M. de Dion's mechanic was something of a genius, keeping the big steam-driven car in operation. The race ground on for almost seven hours, and the De Dion Bouton, piloted by the happy Marquis, proved to be the most durable. And if you want to say it was the fastest, you can—although its speed was 11.9 miles per hour. Two Peugeot cars finished second and third, sputtering over the finish line at about ten miles per hour

To the drivers it was one of the most harrowing adventures of their lives, but to the French public and the press it was considered of little importance. The race failed to make headlines, getting only a brief mention buried in the inside of the paper. But to the new, ambitious automobile industry it was a day of great glory— and the demand immediately was made for another race in 1895.

Auto racing—which was to develop into one of the great sports of the twentieth century—was on its way!

THE TOWN-TO-TOWN RACES 2

When the automotive industry announced that in the summer of 1895 there would be another race, this time from Paris to Bordeaux and back, the French people decided that the industry's ambition had overruled its common sense. Paris-Bordeaux-Paris was a distance of 732 miles! That was ten times longer than the Paris-to-Rouen affair, and it didn't seem likely that any of the cars could hold up long enough to make *that* distance!

But despite ridicule and doubt, plans for the race went

ahead. On June 11, 1895, the ugly group of cars ready to tackle the long 732-mile trip gathered at Versailles, just outside the city of Paris. It was to be a wide-open affair. No limitations were placed on the cars—engine power, curb weight and all the rest made no difference. This would be a free-for-all, no-holds-barred race, and may the best car win!

It was an incredible race, with all the troubles experienced in the first race multiplied by ten. Cars broke down, ran off the road, fell apart running over rocks and boulders, coughed and wheezed and quit in despair, but the best ones made the distance—much to the surprise of the French public, not to mention the car-makers themselves. The race was won by Emile Levassor in a four-horsepower Panhard driven by a gasoline engine. It took Levassor more than 48 nightmarish hours to make the trip; his average speed was just under 15 miles per hour.

This great race—great for its time—did much to convince the average man that automobiles were more than just the baubles of rich men, and that they had some practicability for travel between widely separated places. The automobile was coming into its own

The news of the Paris-Bordeaux-Paris race, unlike the Paris-Rouen affair, spread far and wide. Across the Atlantic Ocean, American car-builders, anxious to sell the public on the idea that cars were here to stay, decided to get into the act. Under the auspices of the *Chicago Times Herald*, a race from the center of Chicago to a suburb—a distance of 54.36 miles—was held on November 28, 1895. It duplicated the French races in sputtering, stalling and general uncertainty, but was finally won by J. Frank Duryea, manufacturer of the Duryea automobile in America, at a hopped-up speed of 7½ miles an hour!

In two years automobile racing had made its mark on two continents—but especially in France, where promotors continued to dream up races and terrains to test the durability of cars. In 1897 a 108-mile race from Paris to Troubille was run. In this one a De Dion, Peugeot and Panhard battled each other almost to the wire. The Panhard, with an eight-horsepower engine, finally won, with its driver, G. Hourgières, coaxing a 25-mile-per-hour speed out of his contraption.

At the time, this was the highest speed ever attained by an automobile.

In the same year another race from Paris to Dieppe was run. This was a 106-mile grind, but is noted in the history of racing primarily as the first race in which cars were divided into classes. There were voiturettes (very small automobiles), two-seaters, four-seaters and six-seaters.

The year 1898 was a big one in automobile racing, because it put two records on the books—for speed and durability. In the long races held up to 1898, the emphasis mainly was on coaxing the car to go the long distance involved, often by sacrificing some of the car's speed. So a debate began to rage. How fast could a car go if a race was held over a very short distance—say, one mile?

Nobody really knew, but everybody had opinions. Many believed that a car, pushed to its limit, would blow up before it even traveled a mile. Others thought that the car would hold together all right, but that the driver might not be able to control it. The whole idea was considered a dangerous experiment, and finally they found a daredevil named Chasseloup-Laubat who agreed to "open 'er up" over the one-mile distance.

To the surprise of almost everyone, the car held up and so did the driver. Result: Chasseloup-Laubat became the first speed demon in the automotive field, pushing his car to a record of 39.24 miles per hour. The accomplishment was enough to make the Frenchman a national hero.

The durability record was set by a twelve-horsepower Panhard in the longest race up to that time—Paris-to-Amsterdam-to-Paris, an incredible distance of 1,073 miles. The Panhard not only negotiated the distance but averaged 26.9 miles per hour in the bargain.

Encouraged by the performance of automobiles in those speed and endurance contests, and buoyed by the growing interest of the public in the new contraptions known as autos, the industry continued to hold races. There was Paris-Berlin in 1901 and Paris-Vienna in 1902.

And then there was Paris-Madrid in 1903—a disastrous event that almost finished automobile racing for good.

During the nine years from 1894 to 1903, the engineering of automobiles (especially their engines) had progressed rapidly. By the time the promoters dreamed up the Paris-Madrid race, horsepower had zoomed to 90 and some cars were capable of hitting 80 miles an hour. But improvement in the construction of the car itself had not known such progress. Steering devices were still primitive and so were brakes. Little was known about suspension and less about cornering qualities. The cars were big and bulky, with drivers, sitting high off the ground, required to keep the car on the road mainly through strength.

What both the automobile industry and the French and Spanish governments failed to recognize was the fact that propelling such monsters at high speed over narrow roads was asking for disaster.

And when 216 cars entered the Paris-Madrid race, this was multiplying the chances of disaster far beyond reason.

The cars in the race were of all makes and types, but they had one thing in common: they were the most powerful and fastest cars ever built. They gathered at Versailles again, this time in the middle of the night, expecting to start the race at about four o'clock in the morning. Despite the unusual hour, car racing had now become so exciting to the populace that hundreds of people gathered at the starting point to see the cars off. Not only that, but all through the night crowds gathered along the course as far as Bordeaux, eager to see the mighty machines roar past on their way to Madrid. It was planned that the first day of the race would end at Bordeaux, with the cars continuing on to Madrid the next morning.

In the pitch blackness of early morning the cars moved into line. Headlights at that time were feeble, flickering acetylene lamps that barely penetrated the darkness. One driver looked at another dubiously.

"If we start in darkness like this, it will be blind driving for the first hour," he said.

Ford Motor Company

Ford's 999 (left) and unidentified car in an race, about 1902.

The other driver shrugged. Like most of the racers, he preferred to pretend that danger didn't exist. His sole interest was in cajoling as much speed out of his monster as possible.

At precisely four o'clock the race began. Cars sputtered and roared, spun wheels and stirred up dust. The crowd cheered above the din of the engines, and within a few minutes the cars were draped like a necklace along the narrow dirt road leading to Bordeaux in the first stage of the race.

Blind driving it was, not only because of the darkness but also because the cars in front raised so much dust that they blotted out the vision of those following. The feeble lamps on the cars were of little help, and drivers peered anxiously into the dusty blackness and fought with the vehicles to keep them on the road.

Adding to the hazards was the crowd of curious onlookers flanking the road. Despite the efforts of gendarmes and soldiers, the crowd was unruly, surging close to the edges of the road to get a better look at the day's greatest automobiles.

The race had not gone fifty miles when the first casualty occurred. A woman, encroaching on the road to get a glimpse of the goggled driver of a racing car, was struck and crushed under its wheels. That was the start of a pageant of tragedy. At Chatellerault, a few miles farther on, a child ran into the road. A man, seeing the child endangered by an oncoming car, rushed to the rescue. There was a screech of inadequate brakes. The driver twisted the wheel to avoid an accident, but not soon enough. The car hit both the child and man, careened crazily toward a ditch, vaulted the ditch and smashed into a crowd of spectators. The next instant the ground was littered with injured and dying people.

Before the 100-mile mark was reached, two more sickening accidents occurred. With spectators lining both sides of the narrow road, one car had a blowout. The driver tried frantically to control the car, but it swerved off the road into a group of spectators. Eleven were injured and four killed. Another car hit a woman trying to run across the road, then rocketed into the crowd and killed two spectators. The car overturned, seriously injuring both the driver and the mechanic.

In the first couple of hours it became evident that the race was a catastrophe. Before day had completely dawned, half of the cars were already eliminated from the race. Drivers would try to pass each other on the narrow roads, lose control, and sideswipe each other—usually with disabling results. Some took curves too fast and overturned. One driver was killed when he tried to avoid a dog in the road and careened into a tree. At least one car caught fire, burning its driver and mechanic as they lay pinned under the wreckage.

But like a juggernaut that could not be stopped, the race roared on. M. Gabriel, averaging 65.3 miles per hour for 342 miles in his seventy-horsepower Mors, was the first in the heavy-car group to reach Bordeaux. Louis Renault, in the light-car category, came in at 63.2. Then, wearied by the long drive and appalled by the cavalcade of mishaps they had witnessed along the way, the two fastest drivers waited for their cohorts to catch up.

They did not know it, but the race was actually over. News of the rash of accidents along the road had traveled faster than the racers themselves, telegraphed ahead to French towns along the course to Madrid. Public indignation at the calamity had soared, and from Madrid had come orders to call off the race. Spanish authorities had said they would refuse to allow the racing machines to cross the Spanish border.

So the race was stopped at Bordeaux, with Gabriel and Renault declared the winners of one of the most tragic automobile races of all time.

Public reaction throughout France was violent. The people would have no more of town-to-town racing. Despite claims of the motor industry that racing was necessary to improve the automobile, the public was insistent that the slaughter on the roadways stop.

Automobile racing, in its very earliest days, was at the crossroads.

PEKING TO PARIS 3

Following the crisis created by the infamous Paris-Madrid debacle, racing took two new directions. A new plan was conceived whereby races would be run on closed circuits where normal traffic was diverted and the crowds kept under strict control. This plan resulted in the heyday of the Gordon Bennett Races in Europe and the Vanderbilt Cup Races in America.

The other direction taken by racing was the long-endurance contest, where speed was minimized and the durability of the car was paramount. Unlike Paris-Rouen, Paris-Bordeaux-Paris, and the other town-to-town events, the new endurance contests were much greater in scope. These races were from continent to continent!

It was in January, 1907, that a conference of editors was held in the offices of the Paris newspaper *Paris Matin*. The editors wanted to increase the circulation of the paper, and they were exploring ideas that might get them more readers. Finally one of the editors snapped his fingers.

"I've got it!" he exclaimed. "Why don't we promote an automobile race clear across two continents—say, from Peking to Paris?"

The other editors looked doubtful.

"You remember Paris to Madrid, don't you?" said one. "We don't want to be connected with anything like that."

"But this one would be different," insisted the first man. "This would be a contest of endurance. Speed would be de-emphasized. Maybe only one or two cars would even finish the race. But as promoters, we would reap all the editorial benefit."

The more the editors discussed the idea, the better it sounded, and finally, in early February, 1907, the *Paris Matin* announced the race and asked for entries. The race would be over existing roads, over deserts where no roads existed, and through rugged mountains; it would be the ultimate test for auto pioneers, the paper said—a chance to test, once and for all, the mechanical feasibility of the automobile.

Painstakingly, a route was laid out. The race would start in Peking, China, and from that point move into Mongolia. The competing cars would cross the Gobi Desert to Kiachta, a town on the border of Siberia. They would then follow the Trans-Siberian Railroad to the Ural Mountains of Russia, travel through Nizhni Novgorod to Moscow and then continue through Germany and Belguim and into France. The finish line would be in front of the *Paris Matin* building in Paris.

It was estimated that the route would run between

8,000 and 9,000 miles. It would represent the most ambitious project yet undertaken by man and car.

Organizing the event took many months. It was necessary to transport fuel and spare parts by camel caravan from Peking to various stops in Siberia. Temporary gas stations had to be set up at intervals along the barren route. Hundreds of tires, which were expected to wear out fast over the rough terrain, were shipped to key spots along the route. The cars entered in the race were transported by train to Peking—and these were the first cars ever to appear in the Chinese capital!

Finally, on June 10, 1907, the race got underway. There were five entries with various specifications. The French had three cars in the race. There were two 10-horsepower two-cylinder De Dion Boutons with top speeds of only 25 and 28 miles per hour. They were driven by M. Cormier and M. Colignon. The third entry from France was a six-horsepower Contal—a *tricycle* driven by Augustin Pons, a gentleman who thought four-wheel vehicles were too difficult to handle.

Holland sent a 15-horsepower Spyker, which weighed in at 3,100 pounds and was a toughly built machine with plenty of durability. This car was to be piloted by a man named Mynheer Godard.

And Italy came in with an Itala, which weighed two tons, boasted a four-cylinder engine and a top speed of fifty miles an hour. It was to be driven by Prince Scipione Borghese.

The start of the race was an elaborate show for the curious Chinese spectators gathered at the starting point. A raucous brass band led the cars at a walking pace for the first mile. Firecrackers exploded in typical Chinese fashion. And, when the cars were actually turned loose on their own, there was no indication that any of the drivers had any idea about making speed. They had agreed, in fact, to stick closely together as long as the route represented tough going.

What transpired thereafter was something of a nightmare. The early roads were either muddy or sandy. There were streams to cross where no bridges existed.

Cars stalled in the middle of waterways and got stuck in the mud. At no time was it possible to make any speed. Ten miles an hour was about the maximum.

Often the roads were so rough that the cars could not travel at all. Chinese coolies were then used to pull the balky cars over the roads with ropes. At other times, Chinese peasants offered mules and horses to pull the stalled machines—for a price, of course.

Over the muddy and boulder-strewn roads the coolies and their livestock hauled the cars, and before long they were competing with each other to see who could pull the cars fastest and farthest in a day. At last the cars reached the Mongolian steppes, west of the city of Kalgan, where the ground was hard and firm and flat. Here the cars operated under their own power. The Itala proved the fastest over flat terrain, getting up to 30 miles per hour. The others lagged behind.

Prince Borghese, driver of the Itala, felt quite smug, knowing that with any kind of luck he would get to Paris long before any of the others. He had the fastest car.

But even the flatlands proved to have hazards. At one point a herd of wild ponies rushed the cars, and just when it seemed that all would be crushed beneath the stampede the ponies veered away from the strange metal beasts, avoiding contact.

Finally the cars reached the Gobi Desert. This vast stretch of wasteland turned out to be a problem for both cars and men. Part of the Gobi is a salt bed, glistening white and almost as slippery as ice. The cars slipped and slid along the slick surface. The glare from the salt blinded the drivers. The sun was an implacable enemy, pouring its torrid rays down on the cavalcade of cars and men. The cars promptly overheated; the drivers suffered beneath the hot rays. Each car carried water, but the thirsty drivers drank it so rapidly that they feared they would run out and be stranded on the fiery sands.

The objective, at the other end of the Gobi, was a town named Udde. At this point a station had been set up where the cars could replenish their gas tanks and the men could find shelter. But reaching this remote town was a difficult task.

At one point the Frenchmen driving the De Dion Boutons passed the Spyker, which was sputtering along, evidently in trouble. Mynheer Godard, driver of the Spyker, waved a hand.

"I may be out of gas!" he called.

The French drivers stopped. This was a race, of course, but you couldn't let a man die in the Gobi—so the French gave Godard enough gas to see him through to Udde. But the Spyker drank more gas than had been expected, and soon the French found themselves short of gas too.

"We will all perish in the desert!" cried M. Cormier as the two De Dion Boutons drove across the wasteland together.

"Why did we ever start this crazy trip?" moaned his partner, M. Colignon.

Then, all at once, the two desperate men saw a spot on the horizon. It grew larger and larger, heading their way, and finally they could make out what it was.

"A camel caravan!" shouted M. Cormier.

"It will do us little good," snorted M. Colignon. "Camels don't carry fuel."

But they did! The Chinese in Udde, suspecting that the cars might be in trouble on the desert, had sent several camels loaded with fuel in search of them. They filled the tanks of the thirsty cars, and on June 19, nine days after the start in Peking, the caravan of automobiles reached Udde.

The next day, under a merciless sun, the cars tackled another flat stretch. The Itala arrived at Urga, the next scheduled stop, well ahead of the rest. At this point, the De Dion Boutons were some 100 miles behind, and the Spyker was even farther. Pons, on his Contal tricycle, was finished. He bogged down in the intense heat of the desert, was rescued by Mongolian cavalry and quit the race.

One down, four to go.

From Urga the road led into Siberia, and the Itala

maintained its lead over the other three cars. But it was terrible going. There were droughts that parched the drivers, rainstorms that almost drowned them and windstorms that almost swept them away. Small boats sank attempting to ferry cars across bridgeless rivers. A wooden bridge at one point collapsed under the weight of the Itala. In some spots the cars had to take to the tracks of the Trans-Siberian Railroad, jarring along over the ties.

But Prince Borghese, in the Itala, saw victory ahead, and he pushed his automobile to the utmost—across Siberia toward the Urals. The De Dion Boutons and the Spyker fell farther and farther behind.

It took the Itala forty days before it was out of Asia and into European Russia. A grimy-faced mechanic looked at Prince Borghese, his heart suddenly light.

"We are in Europe!" he said excitedly.

"Yes," said the Prince. "But Paris is still a continent away!"

It was a sobering thought. A few days later the car reached Moscow, and Prince Borghese and his mechanic realized what "a continent away" really meant. Beaten to a frazzle, exhausted, their car on the verge of collapse, they still had 2,500 miles to go to reach Paris! By swift calculation—and assuming no tragedy occurred—Prince Borghese estimated that they would be in Paris by August 10.

As they stumbled through Central Europe the roads improved. They were in Berlin on August 6. A couple of days later they were in Liège, Belgium.

Prince Borghese and his Itala reached the finish line in Paris exactly on August 10. Crowds greeted them, throwing flowers and treating him as an international hero. The De Dion Boutons and the Spyker ambled in three weeks later.

It was an event that made headlines all over the world. And it inspired still another marathon race the following year, 1908. Someone on the *Paris-Matin*, flushed with the success of their promotion, said: "If you can drive from Peking to Paris, then you can also drive even farther—say, from New York to Paris!"

"You must be out of your mind!" was the retort.

"Not at all. It could be done, and I suggest the *Paris-Matin* promote such a race next year!"

NEW YORK TO PARIS 4

On February 12, 1908, the longest and most incredible race of all time started in New York City. It was a cold morning, with a threat of snow in the air, but some 250,-000 people gathered in Times Square to bid *bon voyage* to six automobiles, their drivers and their mechanics. They were about to embark on an unbelievable 17,000-mile journey from New York City to Paris!

The *Paris-Matin,* still basking in the glow of the successful Peking-to-Paris venture, had inveigled *The New*

York Times into cooperating in the promotion of the fantastic race—a race so difficult that most people thought it would prove impossible. The route was from New York to San Francisco, then to Valdez, Alaska, by boat, and eventually over the frozen wastes to Fairbanks and Nome. From that point the drivers had a choice of either crossing the Bering Straits by boat or over the ice, in either case landing at East Cape, Siberia. Then they would travel over the trackless Siberian countryside to Moscow, then to Berlin and finally to Paris.

There were six cars lined up to compete in this weirdest of all races: three French autos, a De Dion, a Moto-Bloc and a Sizaire-Naudin; one Italian, a Zust; one German, a Protos; and one American, a Thomas Flyer. They rolled on big pneumatic tires, and they were bulging with such supplies as medicine, luggage, food, picks, shovels, tools, automotive parts and firearms.

At 11:15 A.M. a pistol was fired to start the race and the cars roared away, noisily backfiring and creating a din that could be heard for miles. But the noise was more bravado than anything, for some of the cars didn't last long. Just outside New York City the entourage was hit by a raging snowstorm, and by the time they reached Peekskill, New York, the one-cylinder Sizaire-Naudin was ready to quit. As if trying to commit suicide, it plowed nose-first into a snowdrift and the engine died. The car stopped, and nobody could get it going again.

"Count me out of the race," said the driver, in a tone that indicated he thought quitting was a lot smarter than going on.

That left five cars in the running.

Crossing New York State was a nightmare of snow and cold weather. The American Flyer, battling the blizzard, made only nine miles one day, and in another case traveled seven miles in fourteen hours. Eventually the Flyer made its way past Cleveland to Toledo, then took seven days to travel the 258 miles from Toledo to Chicago.

Still, it was the first one to reach the Windy City!

Snow was not so much a problem through Iowa and Nebraska, but mud was. Wheels sank to their axles; cars

1483665

The Thomas Flyer and its crew in the U. S. on the New York-Paris race, 1908.

Italian enttry Zust and its crew, New York-Paris race, 1908

had to be pulled out by their drivers or by teams of horses. Finally the mud so engulfed the Moto-Bloc that the driver threw up his hands.

"I cannot go on," he announced.

Four cars were now left, and the caravan hadn't even made it across the United States!

Doggedly the cars traveled over the western plains. They were now widely scattered, with the Thomas Flyer in the lead, the German Protos second, and the De Dion and Zust bringing up the rear. It took the Flyer forty-two frightful days to get to San Francisco. The Germans, anxious to overtake the Flyer, violated the rules and shipped their car by railroad for part of the distance. For this infraction they were penalized seven days. The De Dion and the Zust came in twelve days behind the Flyer.

"We're lucky to even get here," they announced. "We had to fight off a pack of hungry wolves while crossing the prairie!"

Because the Alaska area was choked with deep snow and impassable, the drivers were instructed by wire to ship their cars by boat to Vladivostok. But with the wilds of Manchuria and the frozen wastes of Siberia ahead of them, the De Dion crew gave up.

"You're crazy to go on," they said to the drivers of the American Flyer, the German Protos and the Italian Zust. "You will perish in Siberia."

The prediction almost came true. From Vladivostok to Paris was an almost impossible trip during those days when roads were virtually nonexistent, and the cars faced all kinds of hazards during the crossing. Often the crews could not find shelter at night and had to sleep in cold cars during the height of blizzard conditions. They fought mud and snow, and their faces became frostbitten. At times they traveled over the Trans-Siberian Railway tracks, just as their predecessors of the previous year had done. On one occasion the Flyer almost went over a 200-foot cliff; on another the same car was almost demolished by a train in a tunnel; and once it was smashed and trampled by stampeding cattle.

But all three cars managed to get through. The

The Thomas Flyer being pulled out of the snow, New York-Paris race 1908

Chassis of a top-winning automobile used in the first round-the-world race, New York-Paris, 1907.

American Flyer was first to roll into Paris, having negotiated the distance in five months and two weeks. The
German Protos was second, and the Italian Zust was a
bad third—forty-five days behind the winner.

It was a fine victory for the Americans, and helped to
place American automobiles in a prestige spot among
the car-makers.

THE GORDON BENNETT RACES 5

In 1900—eight years before the big New York-to-Paris run and three years before the tragic Paris-to-Madrid affair—a man named James Gordon Bennett arrived on the racing scene with an idea for automotive contests that more closely resembled the road races of today. Bennett, an American, had come to Paris in 1867 as editor of the Paris edition of the *New York Herald*. He was a man who seethed with promotional ideas (he sponsored an attempt to reach the North Pole and also was the man who sent

Stanley to Africa looking for Livingstone), and the new sport of auto racing was a natural for his talents.

Bennett decided that races should be organized as international competitions, and he offered a cup to the winner of races run in the manner he dictated. The rules were simple: Each country interested in entering the race would send a team of three cars, sponsored by its own motor club. Each car, from top to bottom, had to be made in the country of its origin, so there would be no claim afterward that the winning car had a French chassis, a German engine and English tires. The motor club in the winning country would then be in charge of organizing the next year's event.

Thus nationalism entered automobile racing with each country anxious to promote its own image by coming up with a winner.

The first Gordon Bennett Race—also called the Coupe Internationale—was held on June 14, 1900, and was run in conjunction with the Paris-Lyons race sponsored by the Automobile Club of France. This made it a race within a race, but the reason for combining it with a town-to-town event was the fact that the automobiles entered by other countries were so limited in number and poor in quality that the Gordon Bennett Race alone would have been a fiasco.

Such noted racers of the day as Ferdinand Charron and René de Knyff of France, the great Camille Jenatzy of Belguim and Alexander Winton, the American manufacturer, entered the race. But it was strictly no contest. Charron's 27-horsepower Panhard completed the run at an average speed of 38.6 miles per hour and led a second-place Panhard by one hour and 29 minutes. René de Knyff, also in a Panhard, was third. But neither Jenatzy of Belguim nor Winton of the United States even reached Lyons.

The poor quality of the cars entered by America and Belguim turned the first Gordon Bennett Cup Race into an all-French affair—which was fine for the French but bad for everyone else. In fact, the French-dominated fiasco might have ended the "race within a race" had it

1903 Gordon Bennett Race, Percy Owen in a Winton.

not been for the stubbornness of Bennett himself. He insisted that another race be held in 1901—this time in conjunction with the Paris-Bordeaux event. This attempt turned out even worse. Only two cars entered the Gordon Bennett phase of the race—both of them French. Only one finished.

Still, Bennett remained adamant. He tried it again in 1902 in conjunction with the Paris-Vienna race, with his portion of the run ending at Innsbruck—a 350-mile jaunt. Critics of the race-within-a-race were vocal.

"With its emphasis on international competition, the Gordon Bennett Races should be major events," they said. "But they are overshadowed by the town-to-town affairs, and other countries obviously are unable to make cars equal to the French entries. One more French walkaway and there will be no more Gordon Bennett races."

That was when an intrepid Englishman named S. F. Edge took the matter in his fine British hands. Edge entered the race with a Napier—the first racer ever built in England. This car was not considered by French manufacturers to be in the same class with the French Panhards. The prediction was for another French victory —and the end of racing for the Gordon Bennett Cup.

The race started in the wee hours of the morning of June 26, 1903. The route was to run from Paris to Belfort (France) the first day, cross Switzerland to Bregenz (Austria) the second day and finish the grind in Innsbruck (Austria) the third day. Edge and his mechanic knew it would be a hard race against tough competition, but they were ready for it.

Edge gunned the Napier right at the beginning and got away to a fast start. But this did not in the least disturb the confident Frenchmen in their Panhards. The English simply were not good car-builders, and the French were certain that the Napier would fold up like an accordion long before it ever reached Innsbruck.

For a while it looked as though the proud French were correct. Edge nursed the Napier along for 200 miles, but suddenly there was a sharp report. One of the back tires had gone flat.

This wasn't considered much of a problem, since flat tires were numerous in those days, so Edge and his mechanic went to work peeling off the tire and inserting a new inner tube.

"We'll have the bloomin' machine going in minutes," said Edge confidently.

And they would have too, except for one thing. When they tried to pump air into the inner tube, the tire pump wouldn't work!

"Dashed bad luck!" exclaimed Edge, beside himself with anxiety.

"We'll be out of the race if we don't get help," moaned the mechanic.

"Not much chance another racer will help us out," said Edge forlornly.

Just then they spied another car struggling toward them. Edge signaled frantically. It was another racer, but the driver stopped.

"What's the trouble?" he asked.

Edge explained that the tire pump wouldn't work. The driver reached behind his seat and withdrew a pump. He tossed it to Edge.

"Take it!" he said, and drove on.

"He must have an extra pump with him," said the mechanic.

"A sporting gesture!" remarked Edge. "I shan't forget it!"

The mechanic was not in the mood to analyze the sportsmanship of the act. He grabbed the pump, started pumping and soon had the Napier ready to go again.

By the time Edge and the Napier reached Belfort, the cars in the race were so scattered that nobody knew who was ahead and who was behind. Edge and the mechanic found a place to sleep and agreed to get up at the crack of dawn and continue the race.

They got up, all right—but when they went out to the car they found it had *four flat tires!*

Working frantically, they tore the tires from the rims and inserted new tubes, then pumped them all up. By the time they were ready to go, they were both un-

Camille Jenatzy in a Mercedes 60 PS, winner of the Gordon Bennett Race, 1903.

nerved. The tire changing had consumed at least an hour. "Frightful luck!" complained Edge. "The delay may have ruined our chances!"

As they drove through Switzerland on the second day, Edge began to notice that his brakes were not holding as well as he would have liked.

"Brakes are fading," he told his mechanic. They stopped, got out and looked around, but the mechanic could come up with no remedy for the situation. Doggedly they went on, using the brakes as little as possible. But it became obvious during the day's drive that the fading brakes were making the Napier a difficult and dangerous car to drive.

The brake deficiency turned the third and last day of the race into a nightmare. It was necessary during the final day to negotiate the Arlberg Pass—a steep ascent and an equally steep descent. And it was at this point that a lot of the cars were expected to fail—and did.

Edge coaxed the Napier up the winding road leading to the Pass, noticing a number of stalled cars along the way. The road was cut into the side of a mountain, with a cliff rising on one side and a terrifying drop-off on the other. It kept climbing up, up, up, and the strain on the Napier's engine threatened to halt the lumbering car before it reached the heights.

But at last the chugging car made it to the top, and Edge stopped for a moment to wipe the sweat from his brow.

"This is the closest to heaven I've ever been," said the mechanic.

"With our brakes the way they are," said Edge grimly, "we may be in heaven before we descend the other side!"

The descent from the heights was murderous. It was the same kind of road, slashed into the side of the mountain. It twisted and turned endlessly, and Edge had to keep his mind strictly on his driving to keep from hurtling into an abyss below. Whenever he looked down into a valley beneath the road, he almost became sick with fear.

It wasn't that he doubted his ability to steer the car

around the treacherous curves; now he had *no brakes at all!*

"I'll have to shift into low and use the engine to brake the car!" Edge shouted.

The mechanic nodded dumbly. He was in somewhat of a trance. At times he couldn't look at the dizzying drop-offs and closed his eyes as Edge whipped the car around sharp turns.

To make matters worse, the road was extremely bumpy. The car shook and rattled, sometimes hitting bumps so big that it was almost thrown off the road—and off the road, in this case, meant over a 2,000-foot embankment.

"We'll never make it," moaned the mechanic.

"Yes, we will!" said Edge stoutly, although he didn't feel as confident as he sounded.

Along the way they passed car after car that had given up the race as a sad mistake. Somehow, they managed to survive the harrowing ride. When they arrived at the bottom, they were sure that only a few cars had conquered the Pass and that they were now in the lead.

"We're ahead of them," said the mechanic. "Let's stop a minute and examine the bottom of our car. Those rocks we bumped over might have broken the frame."

They stopped and got out. The mechanic took a look and whistled softly.

"We're finished," he said.

It certainly looked like it. Edge gazed at the sight in amazement. The entire bottom of the back part of the body had vanished! In that back portion had been every tool and spare part they were carrying—the jack, the inner tubes, engine parts, everything. All of it was lost!

"We've got two choices," said Edge finally. "We still have tire casings in the front of the car. We can either go on and risk a blowout—which would finish us, since we have no inner tubes—or we can put new casings over the tubes we have to help protect them from a blowout, which will take time."

"I'm for putting on the casings," said the mechanic. "But we don't have a jack."

"We'll have to manage somehow," said Edge.

They strained and wrestled with the car, lifting it up, forcing the casings on by sheer strength. When the job was finally done, they looked at their torn and bleeding hands, and the aching weariness of their bodies made them want to lie down at the side of the road and sleep.

But they didn't. They got into the Napier and guided it into Innsbruck—winning the race and leaving the vaunted Panhards well behind.

Over the mountainous race course they had averaged 34.8 miles per hour. It was a great victory for the English —and, for that matter, for Gordon Bennett, for the English win aroused more interest in the race than the French victories had ever done. And in 1903, encouraged by the fact that a car other than a French one had won the race, Bennett issued an ultimatum. Henceforth, the Gordon Bennett Cup Race would become a distinct event. No longer would it be held in conjunction with a town-to-town affair.

Actually, this was a bold move. The Automobile Club of France, which sponsored the town-to-town races, looked upon Bennett as an unwanted intruder on the racing scene. They had a lot of power on their side. The automobile manufacturers worked closely with the club in all phases of car promotion; automobiles were owned generally by wealthy people who were members of the club; and these two factors could work together to make it difficult, if not impossible, for Gordon Bennett to continue his international racing.

Besides, the Automobile Club of France was busily organizing an event of its own—a national Grand Prix, the first of its kind. And the club was determined to build this into such a major automotive event as to make the Gordon Bennett races a mere sideshow.

Nevertheless, Gordon Bennett ran another race in 1903. It was held in Ireland. It was run over a deliberately

difficult course—a circuit shaped like an eight, starting and ending in Ballyshannon. The roads forming the figure eight were narrow, winding dirt roads with sharp turns and many hills. It was considered a severe test of all the basic elements of good car construction—acceleration, cornering ability, brakes, as well as speed.

Edge, winner of the previous year's race, was on hand with his 60-horsepower Napier. So were de Knyff and Jenatzy on Panhards. There were other cars, too— a second Napier, a Mors, a Peerless, a Mercedes and a Winton, the latter driven by an American named Percy Owens.

This time Edge did not do as well. The Belgian, Jenatzy, won the race with an average speed of 49.2 miles per hour.

Actually, the race in Ireland precipitated the decline of the Gordon Bennett phase of racing. After a few more races they were discontinued.

THE VANDERBILT CUP RACES 6

Of most interest to American readers is the fact that news of the Gordon Bennett races spread to the United States and intrigued a wealthy gentleman named William K. Vanderbilt. Now Vanderbilt was the heir to a great fortune and was considered to be among the "cream" of high society. The Vanderbilt name was famous all over the world, and when William K. decided to hold an automobile race on Long Island every car manufacturer in this country and abroad fought to enter the contest.

All wanted to show off their automobiles in Vanderbilt's race, because the mere entry of a car under the Vanderbilt banner was a sales point to be savored.

The date of the first Vanderbilt Cup Race was set for October 8, 1904, and the race was to be run over a somewhat complicated road system on Long Island, New York. The course was 30.24 miles long and formed an irregular triangle connecting Queens, Jericho and Bethpage. It had some natural hazards—grades of five per cent, five railroad crossings where the cars would be required to slow down to ten miles an hour, some sections paved and others dirt, and road widths so narrow that it became a hair-raising effort for one car to pass another.

Each car, according to the rules, would have to do ten laps, so that the total distance traveled would be 302.4 miles. The biggest bottleneck was the fact that there were two towns in the way—Hicksville and Hempstead—through which each racer would be required to ride behind a pilot leading *on a bicycle!* That would not only slow the race but infuriate every driver on the road.

Entries poured in from practically every car-making nation. Among the racers entered were Mercedes, Royal Tourist, Pope Toledo, De-Dietrich, Panhard, Renault, Clement-Bayard, Packard, Fiat and S & M Simplex. Some were high-powered, some low-powered. Some were giants, some small. But all were ugly and all were interesting.

For weeks before the big event the entire city of New York and practically every resident of Long Island talked about the coming race. It was front-page news. And it drew the support and interest of the common people, as well as the wealthy set to which Vanderbilt belonged.

Back in those days a Vanderbilt could do no wrong, but the first race for the Vanderbilt Cup was hardly an esthetic success. It was, in fact, something of a comedy, with breakdowns and troubles haunting the cars from its roaring start to its feeble end.

The first car off was a Mercedes that had a little trouble accelerating. The second was the De-Dietrich at a little faster clip. The Royal Tourist was next, and this one had trouble before it completed a lap: something went wrong with the propeller shaft which idled the car for two frantic hours. The Pope Toledo had to be pushed about fifty yards at the start before the engine caught, and after a few times around the course the steering failed on a curve and car and driver ended up among the trees along the road.

Somewhere along the line a second Mercedes blew a tire, and the driver lost control; the mechanic grabbed at the wheel, and between the two of them they managed to overturn the car. It was the first real tragedy, for both men were seriously injured and the mechanic died before help could reach him. A third Mercedes had to make a panic stop—and that was the end of it. The car virtually fell apart. A Fiat went out with a bad clutch, and a Renault sputtered, coughed and finally gave up after one lap. The race proved particularly hard on tires. They became so hot that it was necessary to sprinkle them with water at way-stations, and most cars had blown at least one tire by the time they had completed three circuits of the course.

What it all boiled down to was this: a French-built Panhard driven by a monster of a man named Heath and a French-made Clement-Bayard driven by the teen-age son of the manufacturer, Albert Clement, turned the debacle into a two-car contest. And what a contest!

In the second lap Heath blew a tire on the Panhard. His diminutive mechanic, who looked like a misshapen dwarf alongside him, took twenty minutes to fix it. Then, on the sixth, another tire went—and this time it took thirty minutes to get going again. Meantime, as Heath howled and shook his fist at everyone who went by, the upstart teen-ager Clement grabbed a lead on Heath and the Panhard.

From then on it was a nip-and-tuck affair. Heath had lead up to the sixth lap; then Clement went ahead, only to fall behind Heath again. Only reckless driving by young Clement kept him in the race, and Heath was on the verge of exhaustion as he tried desperately to keep the youngster off his tail.

Then it happened. A gas pipe on Clement's car began

to leak. Desperation mounting, the mechanic took a hand pump and tried to supply the gas tank with compressed air, but it was to no avail. The Clement-Bayard's engine faltered just enough to let Heath win. Heath's elapsed time was 6:45:45, and Clement's was 6:58:13. Heath's average speed was 52.2, Clement's 51.6. Third place went to Herbert Lytle in a Pope Toledo—an American car that won at least a certain amount of glory for the United States by staying in contention with Europe's best.

Details of the race were front-page news in New York and most major cities across the nation. The *New York Times* devoted a great amount of space to the race, but criticized the fact that, because of the long stretches of road, the course was not visible at all points from the stands and for long periods of time there was "nothing to see." It vouched the editorial opinion that "the contest was not as exciting as a horse race."

Over the next few years, however, the race grew in popularity, and sometimes 30,000 people lined the route to watch the cars roar by. But as speeds increased to seventy and eighty miles and hour, many violent accidents resulted. Finally, in 1908, Vanderbilt withdrew his trophy and the Vanderbilt Cup Races were discontinued. Vanderbilt had sickened at the number of deaths to drivers and spectators, as well as at the unstomachable fact that foreign cars were most often the winners.

The first major racing program in the United States had come to an inglorious end.

To all intents and purposes, road racing was dead in America when Vanderbilt withdrew his famous trophy in 1908. There was, however, an attempt in 1936 to revive the Vanderbilt Cup Races. Since the rejuvenation lasted only two years—1936 and 1937—there would be little point in mentioning it except for one thing. Tazio Nuvolari, the famous Italian who is considered by most racing authorities to be the greatest racing driver of all time, participated in the 1936 race—and therein lies one of the most poignant and heartrending racing stories of our time.

George Vanderbilt, a nephew of William K. Vanderbilt, was the man who decided to restore the races under the Vanderbilt banner. The route was not the same as that used by the old races—the new race was to be held at the Roosevelt Raceway, an old aerodrome on which a special track with multiple curves and only one decent straightaway had been built. But the rejuvenated race was similar to the old races in the sense that the best drivers and best cars in the world were invited to participate. And among those invited was Tazio Nuvolari.

Normally, Nuvolari would have leaped at the chance to go to America and race for the first time in the New World, but he was so beset with trouble at the time he received the invitation that he was inclined to turn it down.

"How can I go," he asked, "with Giorgio so ill?"

Giorgio was Nuvolari's young son—one of three children of Tazio and Carolina Nuvolari. Young Giorgio was gravely ill with pericarditis—an inflammation of the sac enclosing the heart—and the doctor had already told the Nuvolaris that the child would die. It was only a matter of time. No one knew when it would happen.

Nuvolari could easily have made the decision not to race in the United States had it not been for Giorgio's persuasion. The young boy admired his father and kept asking him when he was going to "win in America."

"If I go," said Nuvolari, "I will win a big cup and bring it back to you."

There were other pressures applied to Nuvolari, too. His other son wanted him to go and "win in America." The builders of the Italian Ferraris and Alfa Romeos had merged some years before, and they wanted to send Nuvolari, Giuseppe Farina and Antonio Brivio—all top-flight drivers—to assure an Italian victory in America. Finally, convincing himself that Giorgio would be able to hold out until his return, Tazio Nuvolari decided to enter the race. Perhaps the stimulation of a win in the American race would even help the boy.

Nuvolari sailed from Genoa on the liner *Rex*, along with Farina, Brivio, the racing cars and officials and mechanics of the Ferrari-Alfa Romeo team. While en

Bosch-Archiv

Tazio Nuvolari in 1930.

route to New York he received a cablegram with sad news—Giorgio had died.

Heartbroken, Tazio Nuvolari felt ten years older. For the rest of the sea voyage he remained secluded in his cabin, seeing no one and talking only when he could not avoid it. When he arrived in New York he went through the greetings from fans, the questions of newspaper reporters and the many other things that happen to a sports hero, as if in a trance.

And then, at last, the day came—Columbus Day, October 12, 1936—and Nuvolari sat hunched down in his Alfa Romeo in the starting grid, and once more the roar of engines and the excitement of the race's start began to seep into his consciousness. And he wondered if he would be able to go through with the long 300-mile grind —where concentration was the difference between life and death. He remembered his promise to Giorgio to bring back a big cup, and he gripped the steering wheel of the Alfa Romeo, now straining at the leash to get started, a little tighter . . .

Tazio Nuvolari was, without a doubt, the greatest racer of his time. He had won more races during his 30-year career than any other driver before him—150 races, of which 72 were major events. Among his major wins were the Rome Grand Prix, the Coppa Ciano, Tripoli Grand Prix, Italian Grand Prix, Monza Grand Prix, Mille Miglia, Hungarian Grand Prix, Targa Florio, Belgian Grand Prix, French Grand Prix, Monaco Grand Prix, German Grand Prix, Le Mans 24-Hours, Spanish Grand Prix, Yugoslavia Grand Prix and many others. And he raced until he was 58 years old.

Nuvolari was a small man with a great amount of courage. He was an artist at the wheel of an automobile, and he had supreme confidence in himself. He must have known, as all race drivers do, that he could be killed; yet the courage and daring he exhibited in the heat of a race indicated that the thought was far back in his mind.

Tazio Nuvolari was born in the tiny village of Casteldario, Mantua, Italy, in 1892. His father bred horses, and it was on the farm that young Tazio learned the meaning of confidence and courage. At the age of about five the boy was kicked by a horse, and immediately thereafter began to show a lack of courage where horses were concerned.

Tazio's father decided to correct the matter at once. A few days after the incident he tossed a gold coin on the ground beneath the belly of a horse.

"If you want it," he said calmly, "pick it up."

Tazio bent down hesitantly and grabbed the coin. Courage and confidence flooded back, and never thereafter did he show fear.

He did, however, show an early and increasing interest in speed. At 15 years of age he was racing bicycles. At 20 he graduated to motorcycles, and during an eight-year career on the two-wheelers he won 300 races. The one race that illustrated Nuvolari's tremendous courage was the Monza Grand Prix for motorcycles held in 1928. During a practice run for the event, Nuvolari took a spill and fractured both legs.

"That'll put you in the hospital for a month," said his doctor.

"Not me," said Nuvolari. "I intend to ride in the Monza.'

"Any attempt to ride in your condition would be foolhardy," warned the doctor. "Both your legs are in casts. It's impossible."

"I will do it," said Nuvolari stubbornly.

And he did. He induced two mechanics to carry him to his motorcycle and tie him to the machine. He not only rode for the full 300 kilometers but won the race!

A year later he gave up motorcycles and turned his full attention to automobiles. Immediately he began to show his talents with a car. In 1927 he won the Rome Grand Prix, in 1928 the Tripoli Grand Prix, in 1930 the Mille Miglia, and on and on and on. Newspaper reporters called him The Flying Mantuan, a nickname which stuck. He was also called *Il Maestro,* an Italian title reserved only for the greatest of men, as well as several other names that testified to his greatness. But none of the names affected his personality. He was shy and modest about his achievements, quietly confident of his ability and not inclined to exhibit corny theatrics when he won— which was so much of the time as to become almost monotonous.

Among his many wins were some that were unforgettable. In 1933, at the Tourist Trophy Race in Ireland, he was asked to drive an MG Magnette. The car was completely strange to him, with its unfamiliar gearbox, but he calmly took the car around the circuit once, figuring it out, and then went out and won the race.

On another occasion Nuvolari showed unbelievable courage—if not a touch of insanity—when he beat his rival, Achille Varzi, in the 1,000-mile Italian grind known as the Mille Miglia. Varzi was leading when darkness swept down over the mountainous road over which the race was run. Varzi figured he could coast home, for he saw no headlights behind him and assumed he had a safe lead. What he didn't know was that Nuvolari had been trailing him for miles *without lights!* At the proper moment, Nuvolari roared past the startled Varzi to win the race!

In the same year, Nuvolari entered the Monaco Grand Prix. Near the end of the race his car caught fire, then blew its engine a half-mile from the finish line. Furious, Nuvolari got out and pushed his car toward the finish line, finally dropping from exhaustion 200 yards from his goal.

In 1935 he took part in the German Grand Prix with one leg in a cast. He had to operate the clutch, brake and accelerator with his left foot throughout the race, and he was considered to have no chance at all of winning. But he did.

"I really had to operate only two pedals," was his wry comment afterward. "I never use the brake when I'm racing."

Now it was 1936, and Nuvolari was in America for a revival of the Vanderbilt Cup Races. He was 44 years old. And it was a race he had to win, for a dead child at home . . .

Forty-five drivers had entered the big race at the new

Rudolf Caracciola in a Mercedes-Benz.

Roosevelt Raceway. Despite his fine record, Nuvolari was not a favorite of the American crowd. Mauri Rose and Wilbur Shaw, both fine Indianapolis 500 drivers, were the darlings of the fans, and in addition to these outstanding drivers there were other American stalwarts in the race—Wild Bill Cummings, Babe Stapp and Billy Winn. It was said that Nuvolari would not be able to beat the Americans because he was less familiar with the circuit.

The circuit itself, constructed at Westbury, Long Island, was enough to give the best drivers in the world moments of doubt. Its unusual design made it one of the most—if not *the* most—difficult courses anywhere. The distance around the circuit was four miles. It had a long straight in front of the grandstands; then there was a left turn, the first of sixteen curves that wound snakelike back to the beginning of the straight again. An advantage of the course, as far as spectators were concerned, was that every curve could be seen from the stands.

Tazio Nuvolari sat in the big Alfa Romeo and waited for the starter's flag to drop. There were some 50,000 spectators in the stands, and Nuvolari was not unaware that most of them would be pulling for the American drivers. Nuvolari, however, probably had the greatest incentive to win the race—he wanted badly to take the big winner's cup back to Italy in honor of his dead son.

Nuvolari's Alfa Romeo was in the eighth position in the third row of cars, about 200 feet back from the first line of the starting grid. Ahead of him stretched 300 miles of high-speed driving against not only the eager American drivers but topnotch competition from France, England, Italy and Australia. On paper this was anybody's race, and as Nuvolari watched the starter raise the green flag his lips compressed and he gripped the steering wheel in grim determination.

At exactly 11 A.M. the flag dropped and the cars screamed in the agony of a quick start. A bluish cloud of exhaust smoke filled the air, there was the scent of rubber burned from spinning tires, and then the pack surged forward.

It was at that moment that Nuvolari showed the spectators something they had hardly expected to see. His foot went down on his accelerator, and the Alfa Romeo shot forward like a bullet. With a pickup that left the crowd gasping, Nuvolari's car shot past the second row of starters, closed in on the first row and went into the lead before the pack reached the first turn at the end of the straight!

Nuvolari negotiated the sixteen curves with the expertness that had made him one of the greatest drivers of all time. His "unfamiliarity" with the course seemed not to bother him. He handled the speeding car with such skill that when he completed the first lap and roared past the grandstand, people rose to their feet in tribute —forgetting that moments before they had been rooting for Mauri Rose and Wilbur Shaw.

Nuvolari poured it on from the beginning—and he never let up. He drove with a fury and dedication that was visible to the crowd, the pits and the other drivers. There was no doubt in anyone's mind after the first couple of laps that Nuvolari intended to win this one.

At the end of ten laps—forty miles—Nuvolari had already lapped the stragglers. His roaring Alfa Romeo zoomed up behind the last-place car and, with a screech of acceleration, shot past the startled driver. A little farther ahead he took another one, then a third. At the rate he was going he would lap the entire field—and the race was only in its opening phases!

In those early laps the only challenge to Nuvolari came from his Italian teammate, Brivio. For twenty-seven laps Brivio stayed close to Nuvolari. Then, on the twenty-eighth lap, Nuvolari was forced into the pits for gas, oil and six new sparkplugs. While he was in the pits, Brivio took the lead.

But that didn't last long. Nuvolari roared out of the pits again and passed Brivio before the lap was completed!

It was the only time in the entire 300-mile race that anyone led Nuvolari. The great Italian driver held the lead until the end, gradually increasing the distance between himself and the second-place car. He finished the race three laps ahead, winning by 12 minutes. He had driven four hours, 32 minutes and 44.04 seconds, averaging 65.998 miles per hour.

Jean Pierre Wimille, the French champion, placed second in a Bugatti. Antonio Brivio was third.

Tazio Nuvolari accepted the winner's check and the big cup and even forced a smile for the photographers, and then he carefully packed the cup and returned to Italy.

The cup was dedicated to Giorgio.

PART TWO

THE GRAND PRIX CIRCUIT

THE FRENCH GRAND PRIX 1

Mike Hawthorn

While road racing was enjoying only a short life in the United States, automobile racing was taking a new turn in the Old Country. The new development was European Grand Prix (grand prize) racing.

Before embarking on the fascinating history of Grand Prix racing, let's take a look at what Grand Prix competition is today. The Grand Prix is the absolute ultimate in automobile racing. The cars are cigar-shaped single-seat bullets that represent the last word in design, engineering and horsepower. They are the finest cars manufacturers can turn out, and they are entered by their makers in events that test speed and endurance to the utmost. And they are driven, in almost all cases, by the world's greatest racing drivers.

The races are held on closed circuits, averaging about four miles per lap in length, and they are run over distances anywhere from 150 to 400 miles. Since most major nations hold Grand Prix events, and cars are manufactured in the various countries, a good deal of national pride goes into each race.

Today's Grand Prix automobiles are called Formula 1 cars and must meet rigid specifications on size, weight, engine capacity and type of vehicle. These specifications are reviewed and changed every three years. No vehicle failing to meet the specifications, which are set by the Federation Internationale de l'Automobile (FIA), can possibly enter a Grand Prix race.

Although many Grand Prix races occurred between the years of 1906 and 1949—and many drivers, such as Tazio Nuvolari, Louis Chiron, Achille Varzi, Rudi Caracciola, were considered champions of their day— the official Driver's World Championship has existed only since 1950. In that year a point system was devised to determine the World Champion. The driver accumulating the most points in a series of nine or ten Grand Prix races became the titleholder.

Over the years, the number and locations of Grand Prix events have changed, but in 1967 the World Champion Driver was determined by points piled up in the following races: Monaco Grand Prix, Dutch Grand Prix, Belgian Grand Prix, French Grand Prix, British Grand Prix, German Grand Prix, Canadian Grand Prix, Italian Grand Prix, South African Grand Prix, United States Grand Prix and Mexican Grand Prix. In the past there have been Grand Prix races held in Argentina, Morocco, Portugal and many other countries.

World Champion Drivers, since the point system went into affect in 1950, represent most of the elite drivers of the past seventeen years. They are as follows: Giuseppe

Farina of Italy (1950) ; Juan Manuel Fangio of Argentina (1951) ; Alberto Ascari of Italy (1952, 1953) ; Juan Manuel Fangio again (1954, 1955, 1956, 1957) ; Mike Hawthorn of England (1958) ; Jack Brabham of Australia (1959, 1960) ; Phil Hill of the United States (1961) ; Graham Hill of England (1962) ; Jim Clark of Scotland (1963) ; John Surtees of England (1964) ; Jim Clark again (1965) ; Jack Brabham again (1966) ; Denis Hulme of New Zealand (1967).

All of this started in 1906. The Automobile Club of France organized the first Grand Prix race that year at a nondescript little town called Le Mans. European nations were invited to enter cars made in their specific countries in a race over a closed circuit. Rigid limitations were placed on weight, piston bore and engine capacity. The first race—which was then considered the greatest race ever conceived—was called the Grand Prix of the Automobile Club of France. Six years later it was renamed simply the Grand Prix de France.

The historic first Grand Prix race was run over a long circuit that utilized major highways as well as secondary roads. It had a total distance of 1,238 kilometers (768 miles) to be covered. The race was to consist of twelve laps a day for two days.

Two nations other than France—Italy and Germany —responded to the challenge by sending the best cars they could possibly build. The French, determined to maintain their reputation as premier car-makers, had the most models entered. They were Panhard-Levassor, Lorraine-Dietrich, Renault, Darracq, Clement-Bayard, Vulpes, Brasier, Gregoire, Gobron-Brillie and Hotchkiss. The Italians entered a Fiat and Itala; the German make was a Mercedes. A total of 33 cars reported at the starting point on June 27, 1906.

To the crowds gathered at the starting line the cars must have presented a fantastic sight. Since weight of the vehicles was limited to one long ton, there wasn't much to the cars except engines. They consisted, in fact, of engine and chassis, with only minimum room for driver and mechanic. And when the engines were started, the

One of the three victorious Mercedes cars in the French Grand Prix, 1914.

noise was loud enough to frighten farm animals for miles around.

The first man to start in the new classic was M. Gabriel at the wheel of a Lorraine-Dietrich. He roared away in a cloud of white smoke, followed by the other contestants at rapid intervals. To many of the drivers it was a strange kind of race. Often they could not see their opponents; they were either too far ahead or too far behind them. The only way a driver could tell whether he was leading or lagging behind was to watch the signals from the pits. These were flashed to the drivers as they sped past, and often they were nothing more than a blur.

In the first day of the big race the cars took a terrible beating. Frames were torn apart, and water pipes sprung leaks; there were cracked cylinders and overheated engines and failure of brakes. When the cars limped to a halt at the end of the day, no work was permitted on them. They had to start the second day of the race in exactly the same condition they had finished the first—whether good or bad.

The second day was worse than the first. There wasn't a car without something wrong with it. Only the drivers' determination kept them going. M. Szisz, a Hungarian driver in a French Renault, won the race with a total time of 12:14:07 and an average speed of 62.8 miles per hour.

The excitable French, basking in the victory of a French car, if not a French driver, decided that the first Grand Prix was a great race indeed and vowed to make it a yearly event. In 1907 the race was held again, this time in an area known as La Seine Inférieure, later to be called the La Sarthe. This circuit was 47.81 miles around. The French again made a lopsided situation out of the race by entering twenty-four cars to Italy's five, Belgium's three, Germany's three, Great Britain's two and America's one.

But the surprise victor in the race was an Italian Fiat, averaging over 70 miles per hour—and that really started something. The proud Germans, humiliated in

1906 by the French and in 1907 by the upstart Italians, couldn't take the defeat gracefully. Already, seven years before World War I, the Germans had a Master Race complex. The word went out from the German Government that 1908 had to be different. A German car had to win to show the superiority of German brains, talent and engineering.

German car-makers threw everything into an all-out effort. Makers of the defeated Mercedes, as well as the Opel and the Benz, put technical talent to work to assure a victory for the Fatherland.

When the race started, over the La Sarthe circuit, the French again had numerical superiority with twenty-four vehicles—among them, the Clement-Bayard, Lorraine-Dietrich, Mors, Moto-Bloc, Porthes, Renault, Brasier and Panhard-Levassor. The British entered six cars, Italy six, Belgium three and America one. The Germans tossed nine cars into the fray. Benz, Mercedes and Opel were the models.

The race this time was pegged at 478.1 miles and took place on July 7. Thousands, lured to the sight by the strong nationalistic overtones of the race, gathered along the roadsides, oblivious to the danger of speeding cars.

It was an all-out race, with cars traveling so fast that tires had to be changed constantly as they wore away. Finally dedication to their cause paid off for the Germans. Only half of the cars finished the terrible grind, but of the nine German makes only one failed to finish. A driver named Christian Lautenschlager, in a Mercedes, won with a speed of 69 miles per hour.

The Germans proved to be arrogant victors. They hailed the Grand Prix win as a national triumph for Germany. It proved beyond doubt, they said, that they were superior to all non-Teutonic nations. They turned the victory into a political triumph that so disgusted the rest of the European nations that they let the Grand Prix lapse for four years. It was not until 1912 that another Grand Prix was run, and the Germans, preferring to bask in their 1908 success rather than risk a loss, entered

Bosch-Archiv

Lautenschlager in a Mercedes at the start of the French Grand Prix, 1908.

only a small Mathis which was not considered the equal of the other makes entered in the event and therefore could not be judged too harshly when it lost.

Other makes entered were the Lorraine-Dietrich, Peugeot, Lion-Peugeot, Gregoire, Rolland-Pillain, Th. Schneider, Sizaire-Naudin, Vinot-Deguignand and Cote, all from France; Fiats from Italy; Sunbeam, Vauxhall, Alcyon, Arrol Johnston, Singer and Calthorpe from England; and an Excelsior from Belgium.

George Boillot, in a Peugeot, won the race to give the French another victory. This win was repeated in 1913, and in 1914 the Germans decided to get back into the event heavily.

On July 4, 1914, with war clouds gathering over Europe, the race was run. The German Mercedes took first, second and third place. Again Germany acted as if the victory was proof of their superiority in everything—and not long thereafter World War I began. The French Grand Prix was not run again until three years after the war's end—a span of seven raceless years.

But the French Grand Prix survived not only World War I but also World War II, and today it is considered one of the finest of the Grand Prix circuit. Many great French Grand Prix races have been run over the years, but before leaving the French event an account must be made of the one which has come to be recognized as the greatest of all—the wild and woolly race on the Rheims circuit in 1953.

The Rheims circuit is an extremely fast one over an irregular circle 5.16 miles long. The race was scheduled at sixty laps, or 309.6 miles over long straights, wicked curves and two impossibly sharp turns.

Thousands gathered to watch the big race, and the day was perfect for it. The starting time was 3 P.M., and shortly before that time the cars were rolled into place in the starting grid. Engines were started, and each driver, goggles in place, waited patiently for the dropping of the flag that would set twenty-five sleek one-seated racers in motion.

The names of drivers and cars participating in the

1953 French Grand Prix read like a Who's Who of racing. Such big-name cars as Ferrari, Maserati, Gordinis, Cooper, Connaught and H.W.M. were poised for action. In them crouched the drivers—outstanding men like Alberto Ascari, Juan Manuel Fangio, Stirling Moss and many others. And among them was a young Englishman named Mike Hawthorn, seated in a blood-red Ferrari— a relatively inexperienced driver no one on the starting grid took with any particular seriousness. . . .

Mike Hawthorn was born into a race-minded family, on April 10, 1929. Two years later his father, Leslie Hawthorn, moved his family to Farnham, not far from the great English track called Brooklands. Leslie Hawthorn was a motorcycle racer, but he liked fast cars too, and in 1950, when Mike reached the age of twenty-one, his father purchased two cars—a Riley Ulster Imp and a Riley Sprite. The father-and-son team made their first appearance at the Grighten Speed Trials, with the elder Hawthorn finishing second in the 1½-liter class and Mike copping first place in the 1,100-cc. category.

But this was small-time stuff, not the kind of racing that could turn young Mike Hawthorn into a "name" driver. It was not until he drove a 2-liter Cooper-Bristol at Goodwood in 1952 (his first attempt in a single-seater) that his name suddenly became known to the racing crowd. Hawthorn darted out front at once and stayed there for the entire race. Then, in the Richmond Trophy Race, he placed a commendable second, beaten only by the veteran Argentinian, Froilan González, in a Ferrari.

That was the beginning of Hawthorn's budding career. After those initial wins he raised eyebrows all over the racing circuit by entering his first Grand Prix in Belgium and finishing a respectable fourth. Later he was third in the British Grand Prix.

By 1953 Mike Hawthorn had signed a contract with Ferrari, and he raced the Italian car in the Argentina Grand Prix, the Mille Miglia, the 24 Hours of Le Mans and other major European events.

Now he was in the French Grand Prix at Rheims, and he was eager to add to his laurels. . . .

Mike Hawthorn gripped the steering wheel in his gloved hands and waited for the dropping of the starter's flag. He was well aware that he was not considered a heavy threat in the race. True, he had won a few races, but English drivers rarely were ranked among the great drivers of the day—and there were too many big names in the French Grand Prix this year for Hawthorn to be considered seriously.

Suddenly the flag dropped, and the racers, engines whining in agony, roared away. Froilan González, driving a Maserati, leaped in front of the pack. This man had a plan. While all other racers were carrying full tanks of fuel, González lugged only half a tank. He figured to set such a bristling pace in the beginning that some of the other drivers, trying to keep up, would blow their engines. Having disposed of them in this manner, he would then have time to refuel when it became necessary.

Mike Hawthorn dawdled along in fourth place for a while, but on the fifth lap he made a move. He rushed by Luigi Villoresi and Alberto Ascari and went into second place, trailing only the leading González in the Maserati.

Hawthorn grimly held onto his second-place slot and, with the halfway point of the race nearing, waited patiently for González to pull into the pits for fuel. That would be his big chance.

On the twenty-ninth lap it happened. Failing to shuck the other drivers as he had hoped, González was forced to move the Maserati into the pit area. Hawthorn shot into the lead—and González' pit crew was so slow getting his tank filled that it knocked him permanently out of the race.

But the battle wasn't over by any means. Hawthorn had disposed of González, but he was now threatened by three other drivers. The race had narrowed down to four —Hawthorn, Ascari, Villoresi and Fangio.

Those in the know nodded their heads wisely. Ascari, Fangio and Villoresi were top drivers, and Hawthorn could never hope to stay with them. Fangio, particularly, was a threat. At any moment he would make his move. Fangio was the Maestro, one of the greatest of all drivers,

Juan Manuel Fangio in a Mercedes at Rheims in the French Grand Prix, 1954.

and it would not be long before he would demonstrate his superiority over the upstart driver from England.

And he did. With something over 120 miles to go, Fangio suddenly jammed down hard on his accelerator. He whipped past Ascari and Villoresi as if they were standing still, and then he closed in on Hawthorn. Hawthorn caught the dread threat of Fangio's Maserati out of the corner of his eye, and then it thundered past him too!

Hawthorn was back in second place—but not by much. And not for long either. Refusing to quit, Hawthorn, within a lap, stormed past the veteran Fangio again!

The crowd in the stand caught its breath at the audacity of the English driver.

Now it became a race between two drivers—Hawthorn in his Ferrari and Fangio in his Maserati, rookie against veteran!

Fangio increased his speed. So did Hawthorn. Around the circuit they went, neither driver willing to give an inch. Hawthorn wanted to beat the famous Fangio badly. Fangio just as badly wanted to protect his reputation. Both knew that in the heat of such an intense, wheel-to-wheel race, one of their cars might give out—and that would end the battle.

Which would it be?

Fangio passed Hawthorn and went a car-length ahead. Hawthorn roared back and led Fangio by several feet. Down the straights at 160 miles an hour, around the bends at only slightly less, the duel went on—neither would give ground.

Each time they raced past the grandstand the people screamed in appreciation. They were seeing a race which, for sheer drama, outranked any Grand Prix race ever run!

Into a hairpin turn they roared, Fangio spinning out a little, righting himself with a deft maneuver. Hawthorn stayed on his tail. Fangio came out of the turn inches ahead of his rival.

Around more curves and back on the straight, they sped past the grandstand again wheel to wheel. Both drivers were standing on their accelerators, pushing their cars to the limit. It seemed almost inevitable that one of the cars would blow its engine before long. No car could stand up under such continuous punishment.

Around and around and around they went. Often they were only a foot apart, side by side, sliding together, drifting together, racing down the long straights together. The excited mechanics in the two rival pits were almost out of their minds, and fans in the grandstand were holding their breath.

"It has to be Fangio," was the opinion of most. "Hawthorn is a rookie. He can't hope to stay with the old Maestro."

"But he's staying!"

"Yes, but in the final lap or two, Fangio will make his move. Watch and see."

But the laps fled by, and the cars were still battling it out. Finally it was the last lap, and Fangio had been unable to move away from the determined Hawthorn. The two cars headed for the last time toward the dangerous hairpin turn called the Thillois. Both slowed for the turn. Fangio, half a length ahead, entered the curve, slammed down on his brakes too hard and began to slide. His car squealed, and blue smoke wisped up from his tires. Hawthorn, like an experienced veteran rather than a rookie, took immediate advantage of Fangio's unbelievable mistake and slipped through the opening made by the Argentinian's untimely skid.

The finish line was just ahead. Fangio, recovering fast, gunned his car. Hawthorn jammed down on his accelerator. Fangio's Maserati began to close the gap, inch by incredible inch. Hawthorn, gritting his teeth, saw the finish line, the man with the checkered flag poised, ready. In a dizzy whirl he was over the line! Fangio was a split-second behind him!

Mike Hawthorn, the underrated Englishman, had won the fortieth running of the French Grand Prix against the world's finest drivers, and in a whirlwind finish had defeated the greatest of them all—Juan Manuel Fangio!

It was the greatest and most exciting French Grand Prix race ever held.

Fangio in car #2 and Moss in car #6 at the Monaco Grand Prix, 1955.

THE MONACO GRAND PRIX 2

Jack Brabham

The most spectacular—and certainly the most unusual—
race on the Formula 1 circuit is the Monaco Grand Prix.
This incredible race is different from any other. The other
Grand Prix races are run over country roads between
towns, and the hazards are curves and sometimes sharp
corners and often mountainous terrain. The Monaco
Grand Prix, however, is run through city streets!

The city is Monte Carlo.

The principality of Monaco is nestled on the shores

of the blue Mediterranean in southern France. Behind the tiny country, which covers an area of only six square miles, the French Alpes Maritimes rise in green and lovely splendor. Monte Carlo, the major city but not the capital, is a fairyland of pastel buildings that rise from the shoreline into the hills. It is the home of Prince Ranier and his American Princess, the former Grace Kelly of Hollywood fame. Most of Monaco's income—and its fame—comes from the gambling casino at Monte Carlo, where fashionable men and women of the international set wile away their time at the gaming tables.

In the midst of this fairyland setting the Monaco Grand Prix is held—on a circuit 1.9 miles around and loaded with sharp curves and dangerous corners. There is no straight longer than 500 yards, and then drivers have to brake their cars for a turn. As a result of these conditions, the Monaco Grand Prix is the slowest race on the circuit—and if a driver can manage seventy miles an hour over the difficult course he is doing extremely well.

But it is a spectacular race, run in an area that has more scenic beauty than any other Grand Prix event can boast. If you are fortunate enough to have a good view from a high spot, the gleaming white and pink buildings and the blue water of the Mediterranean offer a sight you will never forget.

The harbor of Monte Carlo is roughly horseshoe-shaped. At one end of the horseshoe is the Rock of Monaco, on which the Prince's palace and other public buildings are located. At the opposite end, looking down on the horseshoe, are the pretentious hotels that are packed with people on the day of the race.

The race begins on the promenade along the waterfront, in about the center of the horseshoe. When the flag is dropped, the cars roar in the general direction of the palace, then abruptly make a U-turn and come back on another street parallel to the promenade. At the end of this street there is a difficult ninety-degree turn, and the cars climb a hill toward the casino. At the top of the hill are two more ninety-degree turns, both left and right, and then the cars race past the casino.

After that comes the descent—a frightening series of curves that take the racers down to the seafront again. Here the cars roar madly through a dimly lit tunnel, emerge into blinding sunlight, speed along the promenade perilously close to the water's edge—and then do it all over ninety-nine more times.

The first Monaco Grand Prix was run in 1929 and was won by a man named W. G. Williams in a Bugatti. His speed was 49.83 miles per hour.

That's not very fast, but the wonder is that any car of that year could finish at all. With the curves and sharp turns, drivers are continually braking their cars, sliding them and shifting gears—all calculated to wreck a finely tuned racer. Most of the time only half a dozen cars finish out of a starting grid of sixteen to twenty. Not only that, but crashes are frequent. The course is so cramped that cars travel nose to tail, and if something goes wrong with the lead car, the driver is apt to find several others climbing up his back.

Two examples are typical. During the 1936 race, the engine of an Alfa Romeo blew up as it left the tunnel. The car spewed oil all over the street. Two cars, coming suddenly upon the unexpected oil slick, managed to slide through. But a third car, driven by Louis Chiron, spun sideways and stalled. It was promptly smashed by four other cars emerging from the tunnel.

On another occasion, during the 1950 race, a multiple crackup occurred during the first lap. Giuseppe Farina started this one, spinning out as he left the tunnel. Two cars at once rammed into him. The three disabled cars blocked the road and the tunnel began to belch forth one car after another, until nine cars were scattered around in appalling wreckage.

The most spectacular single mishap occurred in 1955 when Alberto Ascari lost control of his car along the promenade and went down in the record books as the only man ever to deposit a Grand Prix race car in the Mediterranean.

The most remarkable finish to a race occurred in 1933 when the great Tazio Nuvolari came wheeling out of the

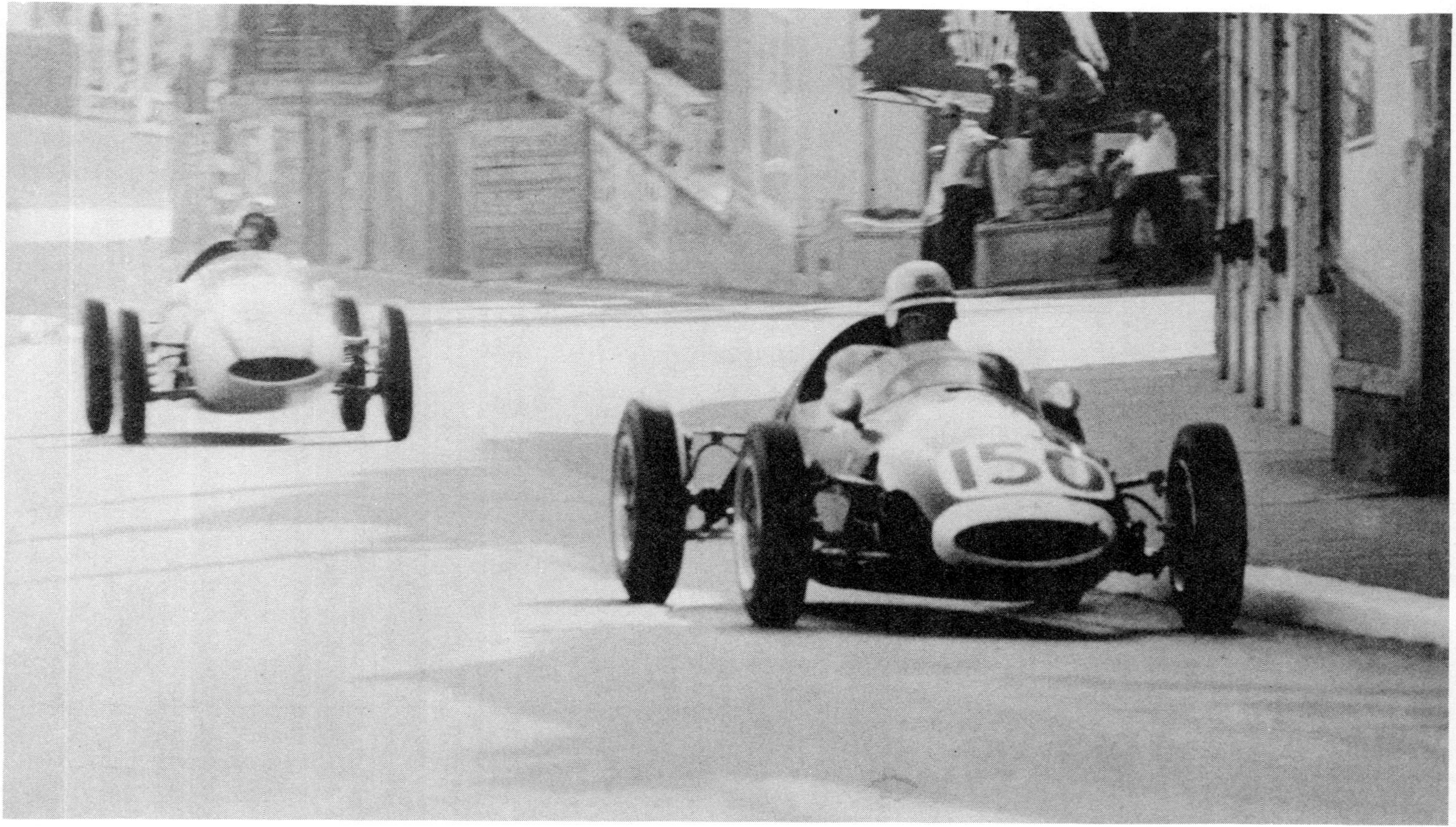

Publifoto-Pix

tunnel on the last lap with his car on fire. He jumped out of the car and pushed it half a mile toward the finish line. Since he had a big lead he would have made it, too, had he not collapsed from exhaustion two hundred yards from his goal. Another car passed him to win.

Probably one of the most interesting races at Monaco was the 1959 event, when spectators were treated to a tremendous race marked by some hair-raising—but very expert—driving. . . .

Jack Brabham of Australia was thirty-three years old when he came to Monaco with a Cooper-Climax in the spring of 1959. Behind him was a reasonably good but not overwhelming record in racing.

Born on April 2, 1926, in Hurstville, a suburb of Sydney, Jack Brabham grew up with a fascination for cars and speed. He learned to drive his father's 1926 Willys Knight when he was twelve years old—in his driveway. During World War II, when he was in his teens, Brabham worked in his father's greengrocery, but this lasted for only a little while. The big war created a shortage of good automotive mechanics, and Brabham took advantage of this by working in a garage as a trainee mechanic. He spent two years in the job, and during that time gained a keen knowledge of what made an automobile tick.

In 1944, at the age of eighteen, Brabham enlisted in the Royal Australian Air Force as a flight mechanic and was discharged in 1946 after the war ended. Shortly after leaving the services he became interested in midget auto racing, but when a friend suggested that he try driving in a race, he shook his head.

"Midget race drivers are nuts!" was his comment.

But when he and his friend built a midget race car, Brabham was finally induced to drive it. And he drove it well. Within twelve months he had captured the New South Wales midget car championship. Then, in 1948 and 1949, he repeated this and also added the Australian midget car championship to his laurels.

In 1950–51 he won the Australian Championship

again and also grabbed off the Australian Hill-Climb Championship at Victoria.

Graduating from the midget ranks, Brabham started to drive a Cooper Mark IV in 1952. He won several races with the car and then bought a Cooper-Bristol in 1953. Between 1953 and 1955 he won the Queensland and New South Wales Championship and placed sixth in the International Grand Prix.

In 1955 he made an important decision. He decided to go to England and take a crack at one European racing season. Then, he thought, he would come back to Australia and run a garage.

But in his first race in England he placed fourth in a Cooper-Alta, and he was hooked. He began to win regularly, and when he went to Monaco in 1957 and placed sixth over the tricky course, he raised a few Grand Prix eyebrows. The Monaco course intrigued him, and he went back in 1958 and placed fourth.

Now it was 1959. Brabham had a Cooper-Climax, and he was back in Monaco to make a bid for first. . . .

Jack Brabham sat snuggled down in his sleek racer in the front line of the starting grid. With him on the front line were Jean Behra in a Ferrari and Stirling Moss in another Cooper-Climax. Brabham was well aware of what these two drivers, and some of the others, could do, and he was particularly concerned about Stirling Moss, a young man who was rapidly making a name for himself in racing circles.

It would be a tough race over a tough course, where not only the stamina of the car but the skill of the driver would be seriously tested. If you could win at Monaco, it meant that you could handle a car with the best of them.

The flag dropped and all three of the front-line racers screamed ahead. Behra's Ferrari got away fastest and took the lead. Stirling Moss was a half-length behind, and Brabham found himself in third place—but right on Moss's tail.

The circuit, with its sharp turns and short straights, made it difficult to pass a car leading the race, and after lap number five the positions of the three cars had not changed. The rest of the pack, however, had fallen well behind.

Lap after lap—along the promenade, around the horseshoe, up the hill to the casino, back down again to the coastal strip, through the tunnel, onto the promenade again—the cars fought it out. And at the end of the twenty-first lap the positions were still the same—Behra in the Ferrari leading, Moss and Brabham inches behind.

It looked as if the opportunity to pass the Ferrari would never occur, but on the twenty-second lap Moss took command. He got his chance to pass Behra and jammed his foot down. Moss's Cooper-Climax shot into the lead.

On the twenty-third lap it was Brabham's turn. He, too, gunned his car past Behra's Ferrari, and the crowds watching the race moaned. Behra was a Frenchman and the favorite of the fans.

The tough race was now exacting its dues. Car after car was dropping out—engines blown, brakes fading, the strain too much for a lot of them. The twenty-sixth lap went by, the twenty-seventh, the twenty-eighth. At the thirtieth lap of the hundred-lap race, Moss was still leading Brabham, having widened a gap of sixteen seconds.

Brabham drove fiercely, almost recklessly, trying to gain on the determined and talented Moss, but he fell even farther behind. At the halfway mark Moss was leading him by forty seconds, and Brabham's dream of winning the Monaco Grand Prix was beginning to fade.

He kept trying, doing everything he could to slice seconds off Moss's lead, but he simply could not close the gap. Both cars were running all out—as fast as they dared on this course of a thousand turns. It was a two-car race, with several other racers trailing behind, and it looked to the crowd as though Stirling Moss had the race well in hand.

Sixty-five, seventy, eighty laps—and Moss still clung to a lead of forty seconds.

Then, with only twenty laps to go, it happened. On the eighty-first lap Moss's Copper-Climax sputtered to a halt in front of the casino with a broken axle. Moss—a hard-luck driver who had had things like this happen to

Bosch-Archiv

him before—threw up his hands. The race wasn't over, though. Brabham's countryman, Tony Brooks, pursued him doggedly, and when Brabham finally took the checkered flag he was only sixteen seconds ahead of Brooks, in a Ferrari.

The win was important to both Jack Brabham and Great Britain. Brabham went on that year to become World Champion Driver and then grabbed the same title in 1960. As to the car, the Cooper-Climax went on to win five times over the 1959 Grand Prix circuit, and it convinced doubtful Europeans, at last, that the British had something to offer to the international racing scene.

THE GERMAN GRAND PRIX *3*

Juan Manuel Fangio

Juan Manuel Fangio sat deep in his bullet-nosed Maserati, his keen eyes fixed on the starter, whose flag would drop at any moment to start the 1957 Grand Prix of Germany. Ahead of him lay the fantastic circuit known as the Nurburgring—a winding, serpentine road system that snaked its way through the Eifel Mountains south of Cologne; a circuit that had 174 curves, some very sharp, to test the cornering abilities of the cars and the skills of the drivers; a course with straights to test the unbridled speed packed into the roaring automobile engines.

It was August 4, 1957, and some 200,000 eager spectators were on hand to watch the big Formula 1 race. Many of them were there specifically to watch Juan Manuel Fangio, for here was a man who had already won the title of World Champion Driver four times—in 1951, 1954, 1955 and 1956. No man had ever won it as often, and now this intrepid Argentinian, forty-six years old, was pitting his wisdom and driving experience against a field of much younger men.

Fangio was not unaware of the competition he faced, but he had clashed head-on with heavy competition many times and he was not overawed. Competition was his life. . . .

Juan Manuel Fangio was born on June 24, 1911, in a shanty town called Balcarce in the Province of Buenos Aires, Argentina. He was the son of Loreto Fangio, an Italian immigrant who had settled in Argentina to seek a new life as a house painter.

As Juan Manuel grew up he found school difficult, but he loved sports and became a good football player. At eleven he had to go to work to earn money for the Fangio family, and as fate would have it his first job was as a grease monkey in a garage. There was an old Panhard-Levassor in the shop, and one day it had to be moved outside. Juan Manuel got behind the controls and started the engine, and it wheezed, puffed and huffed out of the garage. It was the first time young Juan Manuel had ever driven a car.

That was the beginning. Fangio eventually became a mechanic, then began saving his pennies to build his own racer. His first race was as a riding mechanic in an old Model T, and a little later he built his own Ford V-8 Special and raced it. He was good enough to attract some attention, and at last he became a regular competitor in the Argentine Gran Premios, in which he raced Chevrolet coupes and a special Chevrolet one-seater. By 1949, Juan Manuel Fangio had won enough races to be known all over Argentina.

Eventually Juan Manuel went to Europe, working his way through the various echelons of racing until the day, in an Alfa Romeo, he placed third in Italy's tough 1,000-mile Mille Miglia. After that he won many impressive victories—in the Grand Prix of Monaco, Belgium and France.

In 1951 he became World Champion Driver for the first time, despite tough competition in all of Europe's Grand Prix races from such drivers as Alberto Ascari, Giuseppe Farina and Luigi Villoresi. In 1954 he won again, driving a Maserati in two victories and a Mercedes Benz in the rest. In 1955 he went all the way to his third title in a Mercedes Benz, and in 1956 he took the title in a Lancia Ferrari. That was four World Championships, three of them in a row, and now he was about to drive a gleaming Maserati with the lure of a fifth World Championship just over the horizon. . . .

It would not be easy, he thought. He knew the Nurburgring well. It was a tough, exacting course, and you literally had to be a virtuoso of driving to negotiate it. Built in 1925, the road was narrow and winding. The 174 curves seemed to be placed deliberately to test the driver, for many of them were at the bottoms of long hills—or at the top, where a driver could not see them until he reached the crest. Besides all this, the road was usually rough, with bumps that caused cars to leave the road at high speed. It was the despair of maintenance crews as well as drivers.

Inside the 14.2-mile-long ring the ramparts of an ancient castle fingered the sky. It was the castle of the counts of Nurburg, from which The Ring got its full name. Along the route German farmers worked their fields in one area, and pine forests beclouded other sections.

In addition to the natural obstacles offered by the Nurburgring itself, Juan Manuel Fangio knew that he was up against two young drivers in two fine cars who could be expected to give him keen competition.

That fact had become evident during practice runs. Mike Hawthorn, of Great Britain, had lapped The Ring in nine minutes and twenty-nine seconds in a Ferrari, and Peter Collins, another Britisher, had also excelled in a Ferrari. These two young men—Hawthorn was 28 and

Collins 27—were up-and-coming race drivers, and they had good cars. It would be a race between youth and age, youth in the Ferraris, age in a Maserati. The Italian cars were evenly matched, fast and sturdy and finely engineered—and, barring accident, the race would boil down to a contest between the energy and stamina of youth and the wisdom and experience of age.

But Fangio was confident. He had won the last three years at the Nurburgring. This year he had smashed Hawthorn's lap record, completing the circuit in nine minutes and twenty-six seconds, equivalent to 90.23 miles per hour. But six other drivers, including Hawthorn, had broken the old lap record of former years, and there was no doubt that the famous Nurburgring race of 1957 was going to be one of the fastest ever.

Fangio stared at the starter from hooded eyes as he waited for the dropping of the flag. He had a battle plan for the race that he felt sure would give him an advantage. The Maserati he was driving was a lightweight car with a tube frame and alloy tanks. He had further lightened the car by carrying only half a tank of fuel. All the rest of the drivers had full tanks and were going to try to complete the race without a pit stop.

"They'll never do it," Fangio told his mechanics. "The Nurburgring is a different kind of road. It's rough and it uses fuel fast and wears out tires. I'll start with half a tank of fuel and take a quick lead in the race. When I have to come in for fuel at the halfway point, you can slap on two rear tires. That should let me finish the race with-·out worries."

It was a good plan. It made sense. Now, thought Fangio, he would have to make it work. And there were twenty-two laps to make it work in.

The flag dropped like a wounded bird. The throaty roar of engines became a whining shriek. Cars surged away from the starting line, burning rubber as the back wheels spun. Fangio did not get off into an immediate lead, as he had expected. It was Hawthorn and Collins in front, wheel to wheel. Fangio was right behind. The cars roared around the first bend, out of sight of the grandstand spectators.

Hawthorn's Ferrari edged ahead, with Collins and Fangio hot on his tail. Behind them were all the others—famous names and famous cars—Jean Behra and Harry Schell in Maseratis, Luigi Musso in a Ferrari, Tony Brooks and Stirling Moss in Vanwalls.

The three lead cars of Hawthorn, Collins and Fangio lapped the Nurburgring with frightening speed. Hawthorn's first lap was 9 minutes 42.5 seconds, representing 87.49 miles per hour. His next lap was 9 minutes 37.9 seconds, which smashed the old lap record. That represented a complete circuit at 88.24 miles per hour, but Fangio had closed the gap on the leading Hawthorn, coming up with an 88.73 miles per hour average.

On the third lap Fangio slipped by Collins and drove wheel to wheel with Hawthorn. That was when the lightness of Fangio's car proved a benefit—he finally edged ahead of Hawthorn's Ferrari and took the lead. So far, so good.

Slowly, but inevitably, Juan Manuel Fangio pulled away from Mike Hawthorn. He was five seconds ahead of Hawthorn at the end of the third lap, and each lap thereafter increased his lead slightly. He set new lap records on the fifth, sixth, eighth and tenth laps. The Old Maestro —the forty-six-year-old genius of the speedways—was showing his mastery. He was leaving his younger opponents behind him.

Then came the eleventh lap. This was the halfway mark. At the end of the eleventh lap, Fangio knew he would have to pull into the pit and refuel. He jammed down on his accelerator to put as much time as possible between himself and his pursuers before he had to stop. He took every curve at the maximum allowable speed, carefully calculating each curve to avoid a disastrous spin-out, yet taking them without losing precious seconds to his rivals.

When the eleventh lap ended, Fangio went into the pits. He now had a 28-second bulge over Hawthorn, more than that over Collins, who was lagging in third place.

Fangio stepped out of his car to stretch his cramped legs. The mechanics began to refuel the car and change the two rear tires. The seconds ticked by. Twenty, twenty-five. Fangio scowled.

"Hurry it up! I've only got a twenty-eight-second lead!" His voice raised a little in his anxiety.

Thirty, thirty-five . . .

The mechanics scrambled. The fuel was in. The wheels were almost on.

Forty-five, fifty . . .

Fangio was back in the car, goggles adjusted, ready to roar back onto the road.

Fifty-three seconds!

The car whined and tires screamed, leaving telltale black marks on the pavement.

It had taken fifty-three seconds to make the repairs—longer than anyone had figured—and now, adding in the slowing-down time as he came into the pits and the starting up time as he came out of the pits, Fangio was a full fifty seconds behind both Collins and Hawthorn, who were now racing neck and neck. Fangio's advantage had been dissipated by the inept performance of his pit crew!

But Fangio did not give up. His lips went tight as stretched rubber bands across his face, and he poured it on. The twelfth, thirteenth and fourteenth laps sped by. Try as he might, Fangio was unable to close the gap on his rivals. Then, on the fifteenth lap, he began to pick up speed—and this was the beginning of one of the most incredible finishes in Fangio's career.

Not only did Fangio increase his speed, but he used every skill and trick in the book to gain time and inches. He was a supreme driver, and now it began to show over the rough and dangerous Nurburgring. No one was Fangio's master at picking up inches and split-seconds by skillful driving. Hitting the curves was an example. Less experienced drivers, coming into a curve with a maximum safe speed of 95.8 miles per hour, might drop down to 94—and lose seconds. Or, contrarily, they might step it up to 96—and sail right off the road. Fangio would go in at 95.6—just under the safety margin—and gain precious seconds on his opponents.

This is the way he drove now.

The fifty-second lag began to lessen—forty-eight, forty-five, forty. He began to lap the Nurburgring at an amazing 89 miles per hour, chewing away the distance between his Maserati and the two Ferraris ahead of him.

The sixteenth lap. He was thirty-three seconds behind Hawthorn, who now had the lead over Collins. The seventeenth lap—twenty-six seconds behind.

On the eighteenth lap Fangio made 90.29 miles per hour; on the nineteenth, 90.54; on the twentieth, 90.84!

The crowd was in a frenzy. Fangio was driving the greatest race of his career, no doubt about it! He was doing things on the Nurburgring that no one had thought possible.

Fangio's speeding Maserati crept up on Collins. On a dangerous curve Fangio took the inside and shot past him. Now only Hawthorn was ahead—only *two seconds* ahead of the oncoming Fangio!

The twenty-first lap—next to the last! Fangio crept up slowly on Hawthorn. Hawthorn was driving like a wild man, pushing his Ferrari to the limit. Fangio stayed with him, creeping closer, closer—a car length behind, half a car length.

A curve coming up! Fangio calculated it like an expert. He took the inside. His left wheels cut the grass along the road's edge. He went past Hawthorn like a bullet!

Now it was the twenty-second and last lap—and Fangio was three seconds *ahead* of Hawthorn. Hawthorn gritted his teeth and jammed his accelerator to the floorboards. Fangio did the same, trying to pull away, but he couldn't.

The two cars swept down the straight in front of the grandstand—Fangio ahead, Hawthorn right behind. The spectators were on their feet, cheering. Fangio knew they were shrieking at the top of their lungs, but he could hear nothing except the angry roar of his own engine. In his rear-view mirror he saw Hawthorn, right on his tail. Up ahead was the finish line, the man with the checkered flag poised, ready.

Fangio's front wheels hit the finish line. The checkered flag came down. Hawthorn roared across the line, only 3.6 seconds behind!

Fangio had won his greatest race.

The big win in the German Grand Prix gave him enough points to make him the World Champion Driver for the fifth time—and no man has ever equaled that record.

As it turned out, the race was actually Fangio's swan song. At the end of the 1957 season he announced his retirement, calmly and matter-of-factly.

"There comes a time when a man must retire," he said simply. "That time has come for me."

The next year Mike Hawthorn succeeded Fangio as World Champion. Fangio was as happy as anyone.

"He's a fine driver and he deserved it," was his comment. "I'm glad it was Mike."

THE GRAND PRIX OF HOLLAND **4**

Joakim Bonnier

The Grand Prix of Holland (often called the Dutch Grand Prix) is not one of the most dangerous races on the circuit, but the track has a couple of hazards that are special to it. One is wind; the other is sand.

The resort town of Zandvoort, built on top of high sand dunes and facing the North Sea, is the epicenter of the Dutch Grand Prix, the place where the crowd gathers on Whitsuntide weekend for the big race. The two-and-a-half-mile circuit near the town winds in and out of huge sand dunes, boasting some comparatively easy curves that can be taken at high speeds and some fine straights where a driver can pour it on if he must.

But when the wind blows in off the North Sea—as it so often does—it can cause plenty of trouble. It can blow the light, fast-traveling racing cars off a straight course and cause some frightening complications. And if the wind doesn't get you, the sand might—for the wind blows sand on the road and, when it lays on the curves, a fast-moving car can skid on it as easily as on ice.

The Grand Prix of Holland, which came into being shortly after World War II, has had many fine races, but probably the most surprising race was the one held in 1959.

To understand the situation, you have to go back twelve years to 1947. This was the year an organization called British Racing Motors (B.R.M.) was born. This company vowed to build a British machine that would uphold the honor of their country in continental racing.

What they built was a Frankenstein monster that turned on them. Misfortune, to use a polite word, dogged the B.R.M. from the very beginning, and that misfortune took so many forms that the B.R.M. became the laughing stock of Grand Prix racing.

In 1949 the first B.R.M. was ready to race—or so the British thought. But in its first attempt it failed to start; then, when anxious drivers and mechanics finally got it going, it turned out to be uncontrollable.

Men wise to the ways of racing began to chuckle. Those British! They had never been good car-builders, and the B.R.M. was typical of their ineptitude.

The year 1950 didn't improve the British reputation. In fact, no B.R.M. was entered in the British Grand Prix because no driver could be found who would trust the car. It bounced and skidded and rambled all over the road, and it could turn a driver's hair gray in half an hour. Later in the year, when the manufacturers felt they had ironed some of the wrinkles out of the car, the B.R.M. was entered in a lesser race. It poised majestically for the grand takeoff, went six feet and stopped—never to go again!

The chuckles turned to uproarious laughs.

There were other strange mishaps as the years wore on—an engine exploded, a universal joint froze, the hood of a car blew off and almost beheaded the driver, a brake locked and other assorted malfunctions occurred. Then came the 1959 Dutch Grand Prix.

Undaunted by twelve years of laughable ineptness, the British entered not one but two B.R.M.s in the race. One was to be driven by a 38-year-old American named Harry Schell, the other by a 29-year-old Swede named Joakim Bonnier. Neither of these men were exactly superb drivers; neither had ever won a major race in any kind of car, much less in a temperamental B.R.M. And, naturally, neither the cars nor the drivers were taken seriously by the racing fraternity. Race followers predicted freely that both B.R.M.s would be out of the race in the early stages.

When the race started, however, the B.R.M.s failed to act like inept twins. Schell's racer ran true to form and was practically out of the race within six laps, falling so far behind that Schell looked like a Sunday driver coming home from church. But Bonnier's B.R.M., if not exactly brilliant, was at least surprisingly stubborn. It was hanging on the heels of the leader—Masten Gregory's Cooper!

Then, on the seventh lap of the seventy-five lap race, the impossible happened. The B.R.M. suddenly shot ahead of the Cooper!

The grandstand erupted. A B.R.M. in the lead? It was unbelievable!

But, of course, there were sixty-eight laps yet to go.

As expected, the B.R.M.'s exalted position in first place didn't last very long. Jack Brabham, driving another Cooper, ripped past Bonnier's amazing car—and it looked as if the B.R.M. had shot its bolt and would now fall out of contention.

But Bonnier stubbornly trailed Brabham's Cooper for five laps, riding in his slipstream, and then surprisingly roared into the lead again!

Once more the fans went wild. So did the B.R.M. pits. Here was a B.R.M.—wonder of wonders—leading two

Aston Martins, five Coopers and four Ferraris! It was an unheard-of situation.

The bearded Swede glanced in his rear-view mirror. Yes, they were all there, right on his tail, following him like a flock of geese, waiting for his car to blow its engine or spring an oil leak or do any of the hundred and one things for which the B.R.M. had become infamous.

Everyone knew the B.R.M. couldn't possibly finish first!

But at the end of fifty laps Bonnier was still clinging to his perilous lead.

Behind him, Stirling Moss, driving a Vanwall, decided suddenly that the whole thing was ridiculous. He put his foot down and began to gain on Bonnier's B.R.M.— little by little, foot by foot. Then, on the fifty-ninth lap, Moss roared past Bonnier.

That looked like the finish. The B.R.M. had done better than expected, but now it was through. There was little hope now that the car could regain the lead. It was another B.R.M. failure.

But Bonnier was as stubborn as his car. With a deft movement he shoved the nose of his car behind the Vanwall and rode in Moss's slipstream. Moss tried to throw him off, sliding around corners, taking chances. Bonnier clung to him like a leech.

Moss fought to get away, abusing his car in the process. Bonnier stayed on his tail. Then, on the sixty-second lap, Moss's gearbox packed up. Bonnier gunned the B.R.M. and went into the lead again!

The fans went out of their minds. The B.R.M. pit could not contain itself. The mechanics went into a frenzied dance of delight.

It was incredible, too incredible to believe, that the B.R.M. could be in the lead with only thirteen laps to go! Less than 34 miles!

Despite the excitement, Bonnier wasn't home free. Moss was now out of the race, but there were two other drivers still very much in it. Brabham and Gregory had crept closer as Moss and Bonnier vied for the lead, and now they were within striking distance of the speeding B.R.M.

Bonnier calculated his chances as he sped around the circuit. He was sure he could hold off Brabham and Gregory if only the B.R.M. held up under him. If only the car didn't blow its engine, lose a wheel or—well, anything!

Then it was ten laps to go, with Bonnier still leading. Nine, eight, seven. Just 17½ miles now!

With three laps to go Brabham was only fifteen seconds behind Bonnier. Gregory was half a car length behind Brabham.

Two laps to go! Five miles! Bonnier grew tense. Surely nothing could happen to him in five miles! Surely, after all the long years of frustration, the B.R.M. would hold up now!

One lap to go! Just 2.6 miles!

Bonnier eased the B.R.M. around the last curve and headed down the straight in front of the grandstand. Right behind him came Brabham in the Cooper. The crowd roared to its feet, tense with excitement.

Bonnier pushed down on the accelerator. The car whined like an injured animal and raced down the straight at 170 miles an hour. It was too much for Brabham.

Bonnier flashed across the finish line, and the much maligned B.R.M. had won the Dutch Grand Prix—one of the biggest upsets in Grand Prix history.

THE BELGIAN GRAND PRIX 5

Tony Brooks

Tony Brooks eased himself into the cockpit of his green Vanwall, adjusted his goggles with care, fired his engine with equal care and waited with some nervousness the start of the 1958 Belgian Grand Prix. His Vanwall was one of seven British cars in the race—three Vanwalls, two B.R.M.s and two Coopers—and the Vanwalls and Coopers, at least, had done well during the 1958 competition. British automobiles had dominated 1958 Grand Prix races with victories at Argentina, Holland and Monaco. Now they were poised to add the Belgian Grand Prix to their string of victories.

There was a good chance of their doing this because the British driving team of seven men was led by the incomparable Stirling Moss. Tony Brooks, himself, had never won a Grand Prix race, but the hope that springs eternal in a race driver's breast was pounding ecstatically in his. . . .

There are not many dental surgeons who race high-speed automobiles, but Tony Brooks was the rare exception. Born in Dunkinfield, Cheshire, England, on February 25, 1932, he grew up in the town, became a dental surgeon and opened offices there. Unlike many drivers, he was not a true professional at the wheel—he raced as a hobby.

Young Brooks no doubt received his interest in racing from his father, who was a great racing fan. When his father gave him a much used and slightly abused Healy, Tony took the car to Goodwood and raced it. He finished eighth.

An eighth-place finish wasn't at all bad for a new race driver, and a private owner asked him if he wanted to drive a Frazer Nash in another race. Brooks jumped at the opportunity. He jumped again in 1954 when he was invited to drive an Aston Martin.

Brooks piloted the Aston Martin at Le Mans. He drove a Connaught at Aintree, England. His driving skill and deftness improved rapidly, and it was not long before he was given a Formula 1 car to drive at Syracuse. When he won his first Formula 1 race, he found himself instantly famous.

There were other races, then, that helped to build Tony's reputation, and now he was poised to add the 1958 Belgian Grand Prix to his list of wins. . . .

There was only one thing certain about the Belgian Grand Prix in 1958—it was going to be a fast race. The tricky Spa-Francorchamps circuit, named after two Belgian towns deep in the Ardennes Forest, measures 8.7 miles in length, is roughly shaped like a triangle and has thirty curves. One of these is a frightening hairpin turn, but the rest are easier to negotiate at high speed, and as

Tony Brooks—who won his first Grand Prix in Belgium in 1958, comes up a winner in Grand Prix of Germany the following year.

a result the Belgian Grand Prix is the fastest on the European circuit. It's possible to lap the course at a speed of 140 miles per hour. But because it is an "easy" course—meaning that most of the curves can be taken at well over 100 miles an hour—it is also a dangerous one. The easy curves tempt drivers to take them at maximum speed, or even to take them a little faster than maximum, and the result is often an accident.

The Belgian Grand Prix had been selected as the 1958 Grand Prix d'Europe—top race of the year—by the Federation Internationale Automobile, which added an extra fillip to the competition. Nineteen cars started in the race, and when the starter's flag dropped there was a crescendo of engine noise and tire screams as the cars got under way.

Tony Brooks' toe smashed down on his accelerator. As might be expected, the experienced and near-perfect driver, Stirling Moss, swept into an immediate lead—but Brooks trailed him closely. There was a downhill swoop, a bridge over the Eau Rouge and an uphill climb immediately following the start—and as the two Vanwalls of Moss and Brooks negotiated this difficult dip they looked like two green bugs tied together. Behind them came three Ferraris, and behind those several Maseratis. The rest of the field was scattered haphazardly behind.

For the first three or four minutes Moss led the parade, driving with the great skill that comes with experience and is the result of perfect coordination and a fine knowledge of the machine beneath him. But then he made a rare mistake. On a curve he changed from fourth to fifth gear—and missed by a split second. The gearbox tightened, and Moss, disappointed, eased his way to the pits.

He was out of the race, and Brooks had taken the lead. Right behind him was Peter Collins in a Ferrari.

Brooks took curves at the fastest speed he dared as he rounded the circuit, but he could not shake the stubborn Collins. And during the second lap Collins startled Brooks by passing him on the inside. Mike Hawthorn in another Ferrari came up behind Brooks, and there he was sandwiched neatly between two Ferraris.

Brooks and Collins battled bitterly for the lead during

the next two laps. On the third lap Brooks took the front spot; on the fourth lap the lead went to Collins again. Then, quite suddenly, the duel between the two cars ended when Collins' engine overheated and he was forced from the race. Brooks forged ahead.

But the battle wasn't over for Brooks. In his rear-view mirror he could see Hawthorn's Ferrari coming up fast in second place. Desperately, Brooks accelerated. The Vanwall almost took off from under him. He began to complete lap after lap at somewhere around 130 miles an hour, and slowly he widened the gap between himself and the second-place Hawthorn. At the end of the twelfth lap of the twenty-four-lap race, Brooks had opened up a thirty-seven-second advantage over Hawthorn.

At this point it looked as if Brooks would not only hold his advantage but increase it as the race went on. He was driving the best race of his career, and everyone in the stands and in the pits was aware of it.

But Hawthorn was a dogged competitor, and he was not about to concede the race at the halfway point. His hands gripping the steering wheel, Hawthorn began to shave seconds off Brooks' lead. It took him four laps to trim the lead by five seconds, and on the seventeenth lap Hawthorn set a speed record for the race of three minutes 59.3 seconds. But even so, with seven more laps to go, Brooks held a thirty-second advantage over Hawthorn and his Ferrari.

On the eighteenth lap Hawthorn trimmed three seconds more off Brooks' lead, reducing the magic number to twenty-seven. But Brooks remained calm. He was aware that Hawthorn was gaining on him, but he was determined not to panic and blow up his car as a result.

The one hairpin turn of the Spa-Francorchamps circuit occurs just before the cars roar down the straight in front of the grandstand toward the finish line. And it was at this point, on the very last lap, that one of the most amazing events in Grand Prix racing occurred.

Both of the leading cars developed mechanical trouble at the same time!

Brooks, in the Vanwall, had just skidded around the

hairpin curve when he noticed a tightening in his gear-box. For a moment his blood ran cold. For what seemed like endless seconds he could not find a gear into which he could go to bring the Vanwall across the finish line. And he knew that coming up rapidly behind him was Hawthorn's threatening Ferrari!

Desperately he jammed the gearshift into third—and it took hold. He roared across the finish line in third gear and took the checkered flag—and none too soon either.

Behind him came Hawthorn, and just as he crossed the finish line for second place the Ferrari's exhaust belched creamy-white smoke and his engine blew up!

Both cars had been disabled virtually at the finish line. Hawthorn definitely would not have been able to go another lap, and it is likely that Brooks would not have survived another lap either.

And just to make the story complete, a second Vanwall then came into view to take third place—limping in and barely able to finish!

But, despite the last-second difficulty with his gearbox, Tony Brooks had won the first Grand Prix victory of his career, taking over for the British team when the master-driver, Stirling Moss, was disabled.

THE ITALIAN GRAND PRIX 6

Juan Manuel Fangio

The First World War had ended, and out of the ruins the nations of Europe struggled back to normalcy. Shattered buildings and homes were rebuilt, the economies of nations were stabilized and the sport of motor racing was revived.

In Italy, in 1921, a closed-circuit track was built near the town of Monza. In 1922 it was the scene of the Italian Grand Prix; and in almost every year since, the biggest race in Italy has been staged there. Race drivers say it is a fast course but a relatively safe one. It is flat throughout, shaped like a boomerang, is 3.6 miles around and can be lapped at about 130 miles per hour.

Despite the fact that today's circuit is a safe one, Monza has a lurid reputation. In the early days death on the track was a common occurrence, and because of these early mishaps Monza has one of the bloodiest records of all European circuits.

In the second year of its use, Enrico Giaccone, in a Fiat, crashed during a test run when a wheel came off. Giaccone was killed. That same year Ugo Sivocci was killed in an Alfa Romeo during a practice run before the Grand Prix, and a year later Count Zborowski, in a Mercedes, was crushed to death as his car rolled over him. A couple of years later a driver named Pietro Bordino failed to negotiate a curve, left the road and was killed.

Much more followed. In 1928 Emilio Materassi, a famed driver of the day, lost control of his car, and the machine catapulted into the crowd, killing Materassi and twenty-eight spectators. Three years later Luigi Arcangeli, in an Alfa Romeo, met death on the track.

In 1933 another major catastrophe occurred. In a race held in the rain, two cars hit an oil slick in the road simultaneously and roared off the track. Drivers Mario Borzacchini and Giuseppe Campari were killed. Before that race ended another driver died: Graf Czaykowski's car caught fire, spewed flaming gasoline over the cockpit and burned the driver to death.

There were several more deaths; then World War II came, and competition at Monza stopped. When the war ended, the Monza course was revamped before racing was resumed.

The new boomerang-shaped circuit at Monza has been the scene of many thrilling races, but one that stands out in the memory of all Grand Prix followers is the unbelievable four-car battle in 1953. It was held on September 13, and thousands of spectators had gathered to watch the race. To many Italians, the Grand Prix of Italy is the biggest event of the year, and the excitable Latin nature reaches a boiling point at race time. People come to see

Publifoto-Pix

Sterling Moss (#14) wins the 1959 Italian Grand Prix in a Cooper-Walker, ahead of Phil Hill (#32) aboard a Ferrari.

hard, tough, cut-and-thrust racing, and rarely are they disappointed.

In 1953 they got more than their money's worth.

Among the great drivers taking part in the Italian Grand Prix that year were two of the finest—Juan Manuel Fangio, World Champion in 1951, in a Maserati, and Alberto Ascari, World Champion in 1952, in a Ferrari. Both had exhibited fanciful speeds during practice runs, and as the cars took their positions on the starting grid, Ascari had pole position, and Fangio was right next to him.

Alongside Fangio was none other than Giuseppe Farina, the World Champion in 1950, crouched down in the seat of another Ferrari!

Three World Champions were in the front line! And behind them were twenty-seven other outstanding drivers, including such performers as Mike Hawthorn, Luigi Villoresi and Stirling Moss.

It was going to be a whale of a race, everyone was sure. But none could have forseen just how sensational a race it was to become.

Engines were started. The cars were poised like dogs on the end of a leash, waiting to break loose. The green starting flag went up, then was dropped. The noise of engines became a banshee shriek, and the cars were off in close-packed formation.

For a split second Fangio's Maserati poked its nose in front, but almost immediately three cars ripped past him—Ascari, Farina and a lesser-known driver named Onofre Marimon. When they reached the backstretch the four cars were still bunched, and when they zoomed past the grandstand at the completion of the first lap, it was Ascari in the Ferrari who led the parade, with Marimon, Fangio and Farina chasing him like a pack of howling hounds.

It was a strange sight. Two Ferraris, driven by Ascari and Farina, and two Maseratis, piloted by Fangio and Marimon, were in a virtual tie.

No driver would give an inch of ground without a fight, and the four cars battled each other through ten laps. At the end of the tenth lap Farina had managed to gain a slight lead over Ascari, Fangio and Marimon.

Supporters of the four cars in the stands shouted at the drivers and at each other. The pits urged the drivers to ever greater speeds. There was a feeling that the drivers could shoot the works in this one. It was the last race of the season, and what did it matter, anyway, if a driver blew his engine? They would have all winter to get another engine, another car. This final Grand Prix race was *it!*

For ten more laps the four leading cars continued their epic struggle. Farina would lead for a while, then Fangio, then Ascari, then Marimon. First a Maserati was in front, then a Ferrari. But at no time was any driver out front by much. A car length, half a car length, the snout of the car.

"This can't go on," the crowd said. "Something has to happen to break it up."

But nothing did. Twenty-five laps, thirty laps, and still no change. Each time the cars roared past the grandstand, the crowd would rise to its feet in loud tribute to the four drivers who were making this one of the greatest of all Italian Grand Prix races.

After almost an hour and a half of driving—at the fortieth lap, the halfway point—the cars were still bunched. When the fortieth lap was history, Ascari was leading by only three-tenths of a second over Fangio! Fangio led Marimon by the same slim margin, and Marimon was ahead of Farina by the same time.

Only nine-tenths of a second separated the four cars!

With half of the race over and the four cars still bunched together, it was becoming more and more certain that something was bound to give—and soon. Fate would step in and deal someone a deadly blow—an accident, car failure, something. And fate did just that.

After completing the halfway point, Marimon's Maserati went out of control on a curve and spun out. Marimon was off the road before he could bring the car under control, and he knew, instinctively, that he had damaged the car. He went into the pits and lost more than five minutes while a frantic inspection took place. When he came out of the pits again, he was in thirteenth place— too far back to ever hope to catch the leaders.

With no one else threatening, it was now a three-car race—Fangio in his Maserati, Ascari and Farina in Ferraris.

On the sixtieth lap the three leaders caught up to a couple of laggards, Hawthorn and Villoresi, and lapped them. That placed five cars in a tightly packed bunch, a situation that was highly dangerous to everyone. But the danger lasted only minutes before Fangio, Ascari and Farina were ahead of the pack again, still battling for the lead.

Ten more laps went by in the eighty-lap race, and the end was nearing. Still, there was no clear victor in sight. The three cars were practically wheel to wheel.

On the seventy-first lap Ascari managed to edge out front, with Farina and Fangio right behind him in second and third place. Ascari had only a tissue-thin lead, and lap after lap slid by with little change in the positions of the three front runners.

Then there were only three laps to go, with the cars still locked. When they hit the timing strip in front of the grandstand to start the last two laps, the crowd roared to its feet in amazement.

All three cars hit the timing strip in a dead heat!

The seventy-ninth lap ended with the cars still dead-locked. This unbelievable race was entering its last lap. The drivers had been pouring it on for over three hours, and now, on this last lap, what would they do? Go all out or drive with extra care? Both, really. Each driver knew that he had to drive his last lap perfectly. He must take the curves at the maximum speed without spinning out; he must hug and cherish every tenth of a second he could gain. One mistake now would mean defeat.

And then the mistake occurred—on the very last curve before the straight leading to the finish line. And the mistake took two of the three cars out of the race!

Alberto Ascari, leading by inches on the last lap, took the last curve knowing he would have to leave it with one

The racers Karl Kling (left) and Juan Manuel Fangio.

desperate burst of speed. He had been in this spot before, and he knew how to handle it. But something—the tension, nerves, miscalculation?—went wrong. Coming out of the curve, he tried to accelerate his car a split second too soon, and he spun!

When the rear end of Ascari's car fishtailed, it set up a chain reaction. Farina, right behind him, was forced to slam down on his brakes and swerve to avoid a tragic collision. He avoided hitting Ascari, but he lost precious time in doing so. Fangio, ever alert, picked an opening, like a broken field-runner in football, and barreled through.

Seconds later he took the checkered flag.

Farina, despite his maneuver to avoid an accident, came across the finish line only one-and-a-half seconds later.

It was a fine victory for Fangio and a most welcome one for Maserati. Maserati had lost to Ferrari eight times in the last two years, and grabbing victory from the famous Ascari on the last lap was a bright feather in the Maserati cap.

It was also one of the most exciting and unbelievable races in Grand Prix history.

THE BRITISH GRAND PRIX 7

Froilan González

After the thumping taken by Hitler's Germany in World War II, it took the Germans quite a while to get back into Grand Prix racing. During the 1930s the German team of Mercedes Benz and Auto-Union had completely dominated Grand Prix events, but after the war the Italians took over Grand Prix leadership.

It was not until 1954 that the Germans again made a mark on the Grand Prix scene, and they did it with typical Teutonic thoroughness. They developed a fully streamlined

Grand Prix car powered by a straight-eight fuel-injection engine, signed the fabulous Juan Manuel Fangio to drive it, and selected the fast French Grand Prix circuit at Rheims to demonstrate its superiority. And demonstrate it they did. Out of a field of twenty-one cars, only six finished; the rest of them blew up trying to equal the tremendous pace set by the winning Mercedes Benz.

The French Grand Prix, that year, was a debacle from everyone's point of view but the Germans, and the German victory cast a pall over the remaining Grand Prix races of the 1954 season.

Nothing, the experts said, would be able to stand up to the fine Mercedes Benz built by the Germans.

It is interesting to note that the only driver that gave the Germans a battle during the 1954 French Grand Prix was a comparatively unknown Argentinian named Froilan González. His car—a Ferrari—blew up too, but González had kept it in the running until mechanical failure sidelined him. . . .

Froilan Ganzález had a brief but exciting career as a Grand Prix driver. He was a balding 32-year-old in the year 1954, but age and lack of hair was misleading. He was, in fact, a big, powerful man with the strength of an ox, and he drove a Grand Prix car with an abandon that was sometimes frightening to other drivers. There were many drivers who outclassed him in style and skill, but none drove with quite the recklessness exhibited by González. Because of his bull-in-the-china-shop tactics behind the wheel, he earned the nickname of The Prairie Bull.

Froilan González was born in 1922 in Arrecifes, Argentina, a small town not far from Buenos Aires. Although his father owned a Chevrolet dealership, he was not a racing enthusiast. He wanted an educated son and sent young Froilan to a monastery school.

But Froilan didn't do much studying. He was more fascinated by the delivery truck the monks used, and was either working on it or driving it most of the time. Always active, he played soccer, swam competitively and raced both bicycles and motorcycles.

González' first race was in Argentina in 1946, and his

exciting brand of driving immediately made him a favorite with racing fans. By 1950 he felt he was ready to test his ability against the best drivers in the European Grand Prix circuit. The following year he illustrated that he had to be taken seriously by winning the British Grand Prix at Silverstone. Moreover, he won over the Alfa Romeo team that had dominated the scene for a season and a half. Even his own illustrious countryman, Juan Manuel Fangio, fell to González' vigorous driving style. . . .

Now it was 1954, and the scene was again the British Grand Prix at Silverstone. This time González was no longer pitted against the formidable Alfa Romeos but against an even greater foe—the sterling Mercedes Benz of the Germans.

It was common knowledge that no one was giving anyone a chance to win the British Grand Prix this year but the Germans, and if you had listed the drivers who were even considered to have an outside chance you would have placed Froilan González at the bottom.

González did know the Silverstone circuit well. It was not an extremely fast course. Ascari had won the race in 1952 and 1953 with 90.92 and 92.97 miles per hour respectively, and only once had this average been bettered. Never had anyone averaged 100 miles over the 90-lap race. González felt that anyone who could handle his car well could win at Silverstone, and he had a strong desire to ride the Germans and their vaunted Mercedes Benz into the ground.

The Germans, of course, had other ideas.

Thirty-one cars were in the starting grid when the flag was raised. The hulking form of González was crammed into the red Ferrari like an overlarge flower in a small flowerpot. Hunched over the wheel, he glanced around at the other starters before the flag was dropped. There were two fine British drivers he had to fear—Mike Hawthorn and Stirling Moss. But the most dangerous—if you used the French Grand Prix as an example—was Juan Manuel Fangio in his German Mercedes Benz.

Suddenly the flag swooped down. Engines screamed and tires whined as the cars got under way. A cloud of

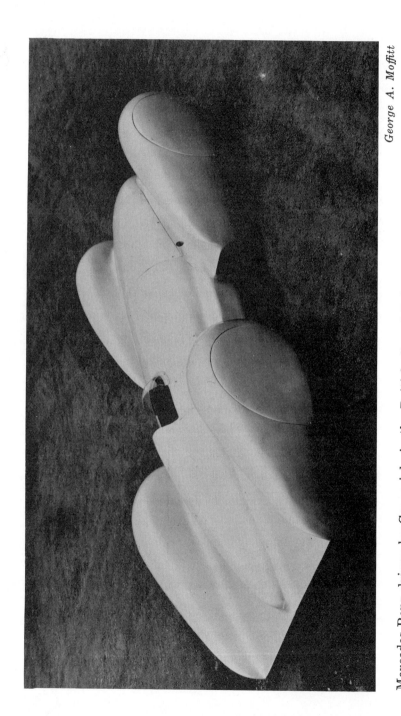

George A. Moffitt

Mercedes-Benz driven by Caracciola in the British Grand Prix of 1938.

blue exhaust mottled the air. And in a body the cars left the starting grid and were on their way.

González, determined to get off to a favorable start, put a heavy foot to the accelerator immediately, and his Ferrari jumped forward like a bullet. As he headed for the first curve, González was out front, with Moss, Hawthorn and Fangio hot in pursuit. He held his advantage throughout the first lap, and when the cars again raced past the grandstand his Ferrari was still in front with Hawthorn right behind him and Fangio and Moss a car's length behind.

Nursing the Mercedes Benz and knowing he had power under the hood he had not yet used, Fangio allowed González and Hawthorn to lead him for four laps. Then, on the fifth, he swept past Hawthorn to take second place —and then concentrated on cutting down the few seconds' lead that González had.

Froilan González, however, had other ideas. Driving with that peculiar madness typical of him, he swept around corners at frightening speeds, he scraped the edges of hay bales, he had his wheels on the grass traveling the inside of curves—and all the time he could see the Mercedes Benz, with the goggled Fangio at the wheel, inching closer, cutting seconds, moving in.

Nothing he did seemed to gain him even a second over the wily, hard-driving Old Maestro and his powerful German car.

González stole a quick glance at the sky. It was a gray day with a threat of rain in the air, and now dark black clouds were scudding over the track. Rain could change things, could produce more caution in the drivers—could, in fact, give the advantage to whoever led at the time. He knew he must retain his lead, add to it if he could, and he went all out to say in front. He turned in one lap of 1 minute 50 seconds (for 2.9 miles), but to his amazement Fangio equaled it and stayed right on his tail.

Behind the two leaders, Moss and Hawthorn were having a personal battle for third place and a chance to move up on the front-runners if either faltered.

Then the rain came—hard, drenching rain that

quickly slicked the track and lashed angrily against cars and men. Now González had a definite advantage—Fangio in his Mercedes Benz had to take the blinding spray thrown up by the wheels of González' Ferrari!

This might have been enough of an obstacle to an ordinary driver to force him to drop back. But Fangio was not an ordinary driver. He fought the spray and the rain as he fought all obstacles—and he remained close on the tail of the Ferrari.

And González, desperate, drove the Ferrari as if the day were bright and the track dry—hard, dangerously, pushing for every inch.

It was on the thirtieth lap, with only one-third of the race completed, that Fangio discovered trouble. Suddenly there was a tightening in the Mercedes Benz gearbox. Fangio no longer could shift the car into third! But instead of allowing this misfortune to throw him, the Old Maestro found another gear and kept racing—and even clipped a couple of seconds off González' lead time in the next few laps.

But now even a more ugly threat loomed behind González. Moss in his Maserati and Hawthorn in his Ferrari were putting on the pressure, chopping seconds off both González' and Fangio's time!

Forty laps, forty-five, fifty—with no appreciable change in the positions of the four cars. Then, on the fifty-fifth lap, Moss roared past the startled Fangio to take second place. And before the Argentinian could recapture his poise, Hawthorn also passed him.

It was now González first, Moss second, Hawthorn third and Fangio fourth. A Ferrari, a Maserati, a Ferrari, and a Mercedes Benz.

It was beginning to look like a great day for the Italians, even though the three leading Italian cars were driven by an Argentinian and two Englishmen!

It was then that González changed his wild and woolly tactics. Still clinging to his slim lead, he suddenly became an impeccable driver. He was no bull in a china shop now, but a careful, methodical driver who was watching the gains being made on him while he kept a little in reserve so that he might rip away from any car that threatened him too closely.

He was completely out of character, but he was driving with the calm of a man who knew he could win.

With only twenty laps to go, Stirling Moss had moved his Maserati within eighteen seconds of the lead. Fangio was now over fifty seconds behind; he was pushing the Mercedes Benz to the limit, but it did him no good. Suddenly the cockpit of the big German car filled with fumes and Fangio was forced to quit.

Tragedy also struck Moss, with only ten laps to go. Something went wrong with his rear axle and he was forced out of the race. That left Hawthorn's Ferrari in second place, trailing González' Ferrari by some twenty-six seconds.

The race was actually over. González kept going and Hawthorn was unable to make up the difference in the ten laps remaining. In fact, he fell considerably behind. When González took the checkered flag, Hawthorn was seventy seconds behind him.

Ferraris had finished first and second, giving the joyful Italians a much appreciated victory over the Germans. And Froilan González, running a magnificent race, had gained revenge on the Germans for the humiliating defeat he had suffered in the French Grand Prix at Rheims.

There have, of course, been other Grand Prix events held in other locations which are not included in this selection of outstanding races. Some have been held annually over a period of years, others withered on the vine after one or two attempts. Grand Prix competition has been held in Portugal, Hungary, Switzerland, Spain, Morocco, the United States, Mexico and other countries. The United States Grand Prix was first held in Sebring, Florida. It was moved later to Riverside, California, and is now held at Watkins Glen, New York.

PART THREE

THE SPORTS CAR CIRCUIT

THE TWENTY-FOUR HOURS 1
OF LE MANS

Pierre Levegh, Dan Gurney, A. J. Foyt

Road racing in Europe and the United States is not solely restricted to Grand Prix competition. Sports car racing is another facet of the game, and it is done in cars that bear little resemblance to their Grand Prix cousins.

It is difficult to say just what constitutes a sports car, for everyone seems to have his own definition. One thing is certain, though: the sports or Grand Tourismo (GT) car does not resemble the utterly functional, one-seater Grand Prix racer. It is instead a two-seater (sometimes four) and is characterized by its nimble abilities as much as its speed. Also, whereas the Grand Prix car is virtually handmade, the sports car is produced in a series by normal (or close to normal) manufacturing methods. Moreover, they are not usually designed exclusively for racing, but for private ownership as well. But they are entered in competition with their own kind, have proved themselves to be capable racing machines and have engaged in many spectacular races on both European and American circuits.

Among the top racing cars are the Ford, Jaguar, MG, Aston-Martin, Austin-Healy, Porsche, Lancia, Triumph, Corvette, Ford Cobra, Ferrari and others. Although technically these cars are designed for private ownership as well as racing, the development of sports car racing where the reputations of the manufacturers are at stake has resulted in the designing and building of cars that are not much different from Grand Prix cars where speed and power are concerned. Sometimes the important sports car races are even called Grand Prix events, but when the name is used in this context it refers not to the type of car racing but to the importance of the race. It is a matter of stretching the truth for advertising purposes.

Sports car racing differs from Grand Prix competition in another important respect. Whereas a point system in Grand Prix racing determines the World Champion Driver each year, in sports car racing the accolades go to the manufacturer. Results obtained in a select group of races each year determine the Manufacturers Championship. These races usually include the Twenty-Four Hours of Le Mans, France; the Twelve Hours of Sebring, United States; the Monza 1,000 Kilometers, Italy; the Nurburgring 1,000 Kilometers, Germany; the Targa Florio, Sicily; and the Tour de France. At one time Italy had a fantastic 1,000-mile race known as the Mille Miglia, but it was discontinued after a horrible accident in 1957.

Probably the most important of the sports car races—at least from the standpoint of prestige for the cars and manufacturers entered—is the grueling 24-hour mara-

The Chevrolette Corvette (#2) driven by Cunningham at Le Mans.

thon at Le Mans. This course is so dangerous that some noted race drivers have refused to ride on it. It is an unholy test of driver stamina, speed and durability that attracts huge throngs each June.

Le Mans is an unspectacular town in the middle of France, about 130 miles southeast of Paris. It is a village planted in the center of an agricultural region and has nothing particular to recommend it except the great 24-hour race that takes place usually on the third weekend of June. The circuit is composed of public roads and is 8.3 miles around. It is a flat circuit, roughly rectangular in shape, and one straightaway, known as the Mulsanne Straight, is three miles long, permitting cars to get up to their maximum speed. Nowhere in the sports car circuit is there a faster track, yet there are elements that usually keep the average speed down. Since approximately 2,700 miles is covered during the progress of the marathon race, drivers are required to stop every three hours for gasoline, tires and a change of drivers (there are two drivers assigned to each car). In the early morning hours, the most dangerous time, there is usually fog, and during many of the races there has been the extra hazard of rain.

Twenty-four hours of anything is a long, long time, and twenty-four hours of high-speed racing is a nightmare. At the beginning of the race—promptly at 4 P.M. in the afternoon—the grandstands are packed with people. Later the crowds thin out, but always return again the following afternoon to see the 4 P.M. finish. Although two drivers alternate at the wheel every few hours, they get little sleep in between. Most lie down as their partner takes over, but usually they are too nervous to sleep. An hour before their stint comes up, most drivers are back in the pits trying to find out how their partner is doing, whether he has lost ground or gained it.

In the mad world of auto racing, Le Mans is a particularly virulent form of madness.

There have been too many spectacular races at Le Mans since the first one in 1923 to mention here, but one of the most dramatic and heartbreaking stories concerned a Frenchman named Pierre Levegh.

Levegh was a little man with a large dream. He was a solemn and serious-minded ex-automobile salesman with a great amount of determination—and one of the things he wanted to do most in life was to win at Le Mans. In 1938 he was signed as a co-driver in the race for the first time, but the car failed to hold up and he was out of the race before he had a chance to take the wheel.

At that time Levegh was close to forty years old, although he had always kept his exact age something of a secret.

When World War II erupted, racing at Le Mans ended. It was not revived until 1949, and it was not until 1951 that Levegh managed to wrangle another ride at Le Mans. By that time he was undoubtedly in his early fifties—much too old to take part in so strenuous and dangerous a race as the Twenty-Four Hours of Le Mans.

But he did take part, as co-driver of a factory-owned Talbot—and he finished a respectable fourth.

That fired his ambition. Now, he was sure, he knew the Le Mans circuit like the back of his hand. The next year, 1952, he showed up at Le Mans with his own Talbot —a big blue car which had taken his last franc to buy.

The big Talbot was recognized by racing authorities as the fastest car entered at Le Mans that year, but there were doubts that a man of Levegh's age could properly handle it. Levegh had no such doubts. Not only did he believe he could handle it, but since there was no ruling against it at the time, *he was determined to drive the entire twenty-four hours by himself!*

This ill-conceived ambition was bound to place a handicap on Levegh, but he did not think so. All the other racing cars would be co-driven—a fresh driver every few hours—and this was bound to make a difference. Besides, some fine cars and excellent drivers were in the race: Mercedes Benzes, Ferraris, Aston-Martins, Jaguars, driven by top men like Ascari, Moss, Fangio, Villoresi and others.

But Levegh had a battle plan calculated to overcome these obstacles. He was an excellent mechanic, and he knew his Talbot was in A-1 shape. Le Mans was a race in which there were always many car casualties. Often, out of a starting grid of fifty-five cars, only a handful finished. Levegh would drive carefully at first, letting others set the pace, waiting for one car after another to drop out of the race. Then, at the proper moment, he would use the great power of the Talbot to take the lead.

The famous "Le Mans start" is different from most races. The cars are parked on one side of the track and the drivers stand on the other. At a signal, each driver runs to his car, starts his motor, and pulls out on the track. Sometimes cars fail to start, but most often the cars are all trying to find a track advantage at the same time—the result being somewhat chaotic.

Levegh almost trembled with excitement as he waited for the signal. When it came, he ran to his car and leaped nimbly behind the wheel. The Talbot started with a satisfying roar. He spun out on the track. He was in the middle of the pack of whining automobiles.

Levegh was fresh and alert. He would not take the lead at once, but would wait for the cars around him to break down. He would stay just close enough to the lead to take over when the strategic moment came.

Around and around he traveled—one hour, two hours, three hours. Eventually the thing he anticipated began to happen. Some of the cars began to run into trouble and drop out of the race. One by one they pulled into the pits, as Levegh and the Talbot rolled smoothly along.

Four hours, five hours, six hours. A feeling of tiredness swept over him, but Levegh gripped the wheel tighter, set his jaw, and continued on. More cars dropped out. Yes, his plan was working perfectly.

Seven hours, eight, nine, ten, eleven. The hours of darkness. It was now three o'clock in the morning. His headlamps cut twin paths through the murky blackness. The road, lighted by the headlamps, rushed toward the car and disappeared beneath it. Straights, curves, sharp turns, came toward him.

Levegh was weary and bone-tired. In the pitch blackness he roared around the track, alert despite his weariness, for he knew that the time was now approaching when he would sweep into the lead—when the one car ahead of him, pushed to the limit, would develop engine trouble, blow a tire or in some way falter. Then Levegh would make his move.

And it happened, just as he had planned. The lead car sputtered, backfired and pulled to the side of the road. The weariness vanished suddenly. The Talbot shot past the stalled car. Levegh was in the lead!

The dark hours continued. The morning fog moved in. Then the sun burned through the mist and there was daylight again. During those dangerous morning hours, when the gray fog was the heaviest, the intrepid Levegh built himself an impressive lead. By the time the sun had seered the fog away, the race had dwindled to five cars— Levegh's Talbot, two Mercedes Benzes, an Aston-Martin and a Ferrari.

And Levegh led them all by four laps— thirty-two miles!

Early in the morning Levegh pulled into the pit for fuel. As the mechanics worked over the car, a co-driver who was on hand to relieve Levegh if he wanted it began to plead with him.

"You've got it won, Pierre! A fresh driver will help you put it away!"

Levegh shook his head. His face was pale, his eyes half-closed.

"I will do it myself!"

The word, of course, reached the grandstand. The crowds, assembling again for the daylight finish of the race, buzzed with the fantastic news that Levegh was going to drive the entire race alone.

"He'll never do it! He's over fifty years old!"

"But if he does, it will be a great victory for the French. Imagine a fifty-year-old man beating the German Mercedes Benzes! *Mon Dieu*, how the Germans will squirm!"

Levegh climbed wearily back into the car and gunned it away from the pit. He was on the track again. He felt elated and drowsy at the same time. The sun rose higher, pouring down its scorching heat. Levegh drove as if in a trance. A couple of times his head nodded, snapped erect again—at better than 100 miles an hour!

Levegh was playing a dangerous game, a hide-and-seek game with death.

Noontime. People ate picnic lunches in the stands. Conversation buzzed. Levegh's name was on all lips. The Talbot pit crew shook their heads in disbelief.

Four more torture-filled hours to go!

Levegh swept into the pits again. He needed fuel. The mechanics clambored all over the car, checking this and that. His co-driver looked at him and shook his head. Levegh's eyes were glazed; he stared straight ahead like some sort of robot controlled by outside forces.

"I'll take it the last four hours," suggested the co-driver.

Levegh didn't answer. Perhaps he didn't hear. He drove away from the pit area at a slow pace, much slower than before. The pit crew knew what was happening. His laps were growing slower and slower. He was squandering his lead. But the lead had been so big that maybe he could still hold it.

Maybe.

Three hours to go, two, one!

Levegh drove by instinct, still lapping the course at 100 miles an hour, enough to protect his lead. But at 100 miles an hour, an instant of inattention could result in an accident and death. Levegh seemed unaware of this. Before him dangled the glory he had sought all his life—a big win at Le Mans—and he was determined to make it all alone.

"He'll never do it!" said the co-driver.

"The man's out of his mind!"

"He looked like a walking corpse when he came in last time."

"But he might do it. He just might. There's less than an hour to go now."

The official timer's clock said ten past three. Only fifty minutes to go! Levegh, snuggled down in the cockpit of the Talbot, almost smiled. Yes, he could do it. It would be torture, but he could do it. Stay awake fifty minutes more. That's all. Keep going around and around, like a man hypnotized. Stave off exhaustion for fifty minutes more.

The race was all his. Despite his creeping exhaustion, he was ahead of the second-place Mercedes Benz by twenty-five miles. The other Mercedes Benz was thirty-five miles back. He could coast home now. Just keep the car on the track, keep his head from lolling from side to side, keep his heavy-lidded eyes open, his senses as alert as possible.

And then, on a curve, it happened. His befuddled mind had almost deserted him, and, with no awareness of what he was doing, he attempted to shift his car up and shifted down instead—and the engine conked out.

A racing official brought the exhausted Levegh back to the pits. He got out of the car and staggered awkwardly. Then he vomited. He choked and vomited for an hour, and when his sickness passed he wept unashamedly in his disappointment.

The two German cars had gone on to take first and second places, and the crowds in the stands were silent and angry.

Later, when the significance of the event became better known, comments were heard about Levegh's stupidity. He had had a chance to win glory for France and had muffed it—muffed it because he had selfishly refused to hand over the wheel to a fresh driver.

He was not a great French hero at all. Far from it. He was a goat.

Levegh's unreasoning act forced a change in the rules of the Le Mans race. Regulations were written that limited any one driver's participation to fourteen hours behind the wheel. Never again would a Levegh be permitted to go the route.

The loss of the 1952 Le Mans race by Levegh after he had built a commanding lead was the hardest blow he had ever taken. But he was a man of towering ambition who refused to admit he was through, and three more times he

entered the Twenty-Four Hours. In 1953 he finished fifteenth. In 1954 he was in a crash that put him out of the race.

Then came 1955.

This time Levegh drove a Mercedes. It was a fine car, and it gave him the biggest chance he had had since 1952. His spirits were soaring again. Maybe, at last, he could do it.

But poor Levegh's participation in the 1955 race was only two hours long. At 6 P.M., the accident occurred. A Jaguar driven by Mike Hawthorn swung into the pits. Behind him an Austin-Healy, driven by Lance Macklin, swerved to avoid a collision and spun out.

Levegh was doing 150 miles an hour when he saw the Austin-Healy skid. He could not avoid a collision. The big Mercedes rode up the back of the Austin-Healy as if on a ramp, hurtled through the air, turning upside down as it went!

It landed with a frightening noise among hundreds of people standing on an embankment. When it crashed it exploded, spraying the crowd with metal and fire. As the car slowly burned, Pierre Levegh lay dead on the ground. And even worse, eighty-three spectators lay dead around him.

The disaster was of such great magnitude that racing virtually came to a stop, with several Grand Prix events canceled for the year. For a time it looked as though the Twenty-Four Hours of Le Mans would never be run again. But it resumed the following year, after millions of dollars were spent to improve barriers and other safety features to forestall another such calamity.

Pierre Levegh had not realized his ambition to win at Le Mans, but had gained a reputation of a sort for having attempted to drive the Twenty-Four Hours alone and for having gone to his death in the worst carnage ever at the Le Mans circuit.

Le Mans has been the scene of many great races. A recent development at Le Mans is of particular interest to Americans. The Twenty-Four Hours, in the 1950s and 1960s, was almost the exclusive property of the Jaguars and Ferraris. However, in 1966 and 1967, Ford Motor Company placed Ford GTs in the race and gave the foreign car-makers more trouble than they had ever considered possible.

The Ford Motor Company actually entered European road racing in 1964 but was not immediately successful. In that year the Fords broke down and a Ferrari won the race. In 1965 the Fords again experienced mechanical trouble and the Ferraris won. European fans smiled knowingly. The upstart Fords from America would never be able to compete with the finely made European cars—that seemed evident.

But in 1966 the pattern changed. The Ferraris ran into trouble and withdrew from the race, and the Fords went on to take first, second and third places.

It was an astounding achievement, and Enzo Ferrari, maker of the Ferrari racers, could hardly believe it. He vowed to put a car on the track at Le Mans in 1967 which would regain the championship from the pesky Fords. The car turned out to be a 12-cylinder, 450-horsepower job with a weight of only 1,875 pounds. Ford's major entry was the Mark IV, with a horsepower of over 500 but with more weight—2,205 pounds. There were four of these, along with two Mark IIs—a total of six Fords in the race.

The co-drivers of Ford's No. 1 car were Dan Gurney, a highly competent American driver who was known in the business as a "hard-luck driver" because he had lost so many races because of bad breaks, and A. J. Foyt, a three-time winner of the Indianapolis 500. . . .

Dan Gurney was born in Port Jefferson, New York. He was a teen-ager when the family moved to Riverside, California, in 1948—a move that started things humming for young Dan in the world of racing. Riverside was a hot-bed of stock car racing, and Dan found himself caught up in the excitement of the sport. He drove a Triumph TR2 at Torrey Pines in his first race, and that was the beginning of his racing career. After that he drove all makes of cars—a Porsche Speedster, a Lancia, a Denzel, a Corvette, a Maserati, a Ferrari. He drove on oval tracks and road circuits and finally broke into Grand Prix racing—

and this variety gained him a reputation in the racing business as perhaps the most versatile driver in the world.

But he was just about the unluckiest too. Many times, when he was leading, some trivial thing would happen to his car and he would be forced out of the race. Once a steering wheel broke in his hand—as rare a mechanical failure as one can imagine. One year, during the 12-hour race at Sebring, Florida, Gurney's Ford GT was well ahead of the pack with all the favored Ferraris in the pits. Then, on his last lap, the engine conked out and another car won.

In the Belgian Grand Prix something went wrong with his fuel line and he was forced to quit, and in the 1967 Indianapolis 500 a burned piston caused his ruin.

Still, despite this kind of bad luck, other drivers respected the lean, six-foot-two-inch Gurney and saw in him a threat that had to be reckoned with in the 1967 Twenty-Four Hours of Le Mans.

Gurney's partner, A. J. Foyt, was born on January 16, 1935, in Houston, Texas, the son of a garage owner. He acquired a familiarity with cars at an early age, and at 18 he competed in his first race—a midget event in Texas.

Although he participated in such races as the Sebring 12-Hour, Foyt was better known in America as an oval-track driver. There was a reason for this notoriety. Foyt won the Indianapolis 500 on three occasions—1961, 1964 and 1967—joining Wilbur Shaw, Louis Meyer and Mauri Rose as the only three-time winners. He also posted major stock car victories, including the Daytona 500 and the Atlanta 500.

Now the "oval-track diehard," as he was known, would be participating for the first time at Le Mans. . . .

The Twenty-Four Hours of Le Mans began at 4 P.M. sharp on June 10, 1967, with Dan Gurney taking the first stint behind the wheel. Race fans were excited about the event. They were sure that the big race would boil down to an epic struggle between Ferrari and Ford. Both cars had backers willing to bet big money on the outcome. When the drivers raced to their machines in the Le Mans start, fired their engines and screeched down the track, the fans were on their feet yelling at the top of their lungs.

Gurney grabbed an early lead in the race, and two other Fords stayed with him. At the end of two hours the Fords were running one-two-three with the Ferraris behind them. No one in the Ferrari pits was particularly worried at this stage of the game. It was a long, grueling 24-hour race, and a lot could happen. The Ferraris would stay close on the heels of the Fords, waiting for them to develop mechanical trouble, which Ferrari followers were sure they would do. Then the Ferraris would make their move.

But by 10 P.M. the Gurney-Foyt Ford was ahead of the field by four laps. A Ferrari was second, but two other Fords were right behind, pressing the foreign car.

Then trouble took a hand. The No. 4 car of Ford's went out of the race with mechanical trouble. A Ferrari caught fire and was destroyed. Another Ferrari developed fuel-injection trouble. A third Ferrari went out during the long night, followed by another Ford.

But that was not all. At 3:30 A.M., in the pitch black of pre-dawn, the big accident occurred. Ford's No. 3 car spun out on a curve, hit a wall and bounced back on the track. Right behind came Ford No. 5. In a wild attempt to miss the stalled car in front of him, the driver took No. 5 into the wall. It also bounced off and came to a stop in the middle of the track. A third Ford then came along and also crashed into the wall trying to miss the two stalled cars.

It sounded like doomsday for the men in the Ford pits. Three Fords were out of the race, another being worked on in the pits, and a fifth far back in the race. Only the Gurney-Foyt Ford was doing well—it still roared along in first place.

Still, the advantage now seemed to be with Ferrari. The Ferrari team still had three cars in the race, and they were chasing the first-place Ford like a pack of howling wolves. The Ford backers were down to one car, and had to rely completely on it.

The sun finally turned night into day, and at 11 A.M.

the Gurney-Foyt Ford was still setting the pace. Where they had at one time enjoyed a seven-lap lead, however, now the lead was down to four. Not only that, but there were now only sixteen cars left in the race—thirty-nine of them had been eliminated!

Noon came, then one o'clock, then two. The Gurney-Foyt Ford now led by under four laps. The Ferraris kept chopping away at the lead. The Ferrari team's hope was that the one remaining Ford would blow up, that it would not be able to maintain the strenuous pace it had set for almost the entire race.

But it went on, roaring down the straights at 200 miles an hour, taking the curves at frightful speeds. In the last hour of the race Foyt was at the wheel. It was up to him to bring the car home a winner, and in the pit area Dan Gurney paced nervously.

Hard Luck Gurney was worried. The race seemed to be in the bag. After setting a blistering pace, the Ferraris had finally slowed. All Foyt had to do now was drive it around and around and coast home a winner.

Gurney gritted his teeth. If only they could get by the next hour without a failure. There were a hundred and one important parts to an automobile that might break, collapse, fall off or something. It had happened to him before; it didn't seem possible it could happen again.

It didn't this time. Foyt drove the car home a winner, and Ford had dominated the Ferraris again in the big 1967 race. It was the first time that an American car driven by American drivers had ever won at Le Mans—and in winning, the Ford Mark IV had set a new record for the total number of laps covered (388) and for average speed (135.482 miles per hour).

ITALY'S UNBELIEVABLE   2
MILLE MIGLIA

Stirling Moss

The famous Italian road race known as the Mille Miglia is no longer run. It was abandoned in 1957 when a car crashed into a group of spectators at 150 miles an hour, killing ten of them as well as the driver and co-driver. And yet, even after more than a decade, race fans still talk about the race—and for good reason. It was generally recognized as the *toughest race in the world!*

The Mille Miglia circuit was 1,000 miles long—an incredible test of both driver and car. It was run over roads normally used for everyday traffic and which were closed to all other cars during the racing hours. Some of the roads were good, some appallingly bad. The course was roughly like a figure eight, starting at Brescia, going through Rome and returning to Brescia again. It wound through heavily populated country north of Rome, and traversed such villages as Bologna, Florence, Perugia and even the outskirts of Venice, where gondolas are the major form of locomotion. There was flat driving over the plains of Lombardy and dizzying climbs to the heights of the Etruscan and Roman Apennines.

One of the major purposes of the race was to test the durability of the cars entered in the race, and this it did with a vengeance. But it tested also the skill and knowledge of the driver—for no man, unless he knew his car down to the last bolt and nut and the circuit down to the last curve and hill, could possibly win the difficult Mille Miglia.

There was one driver who illustrated this point better than anyone—the great English racer Stirling Moss. . . .

Stirling Moss was born on September 17, 1929, into what could be called a racing family. His father, Alfred Moss, a London dentist, was a car enthusiast who had raced automobiles with mild success, but enough to have appeared once in the Indianapolis 500. His mother, Aileen, drove in competitive rallies, and in 1936 she was crowned the Woman's Champion of England. His sister, Pat, was an expert horsewoman, and once, when she and Stirling were in their teens, they entered a horse show and won all the prizes between them.

But Stirling's main concern right from boyhood was automobiles. He had an Austin when he was ten years old —to look at and tinker with, if not to drive. He was so anxious to drive that when he was fifteen his father bought him a Morgan three-wheeler—since in England it was legal to drive a three-wheel vehicle earlier than a four-wheeler. At seventeen, when he could legally drive a regular car, he obtained a German sports car called a B.M.W. And at eighteen he got his first true racing car— an English Cooper.

Stirling Moss immediately began to make his presence known in the world of automobiles. In the first fifteen events he entered—hill climbs and races—he won eleven. Before his retirement in 1963 after an accident, he was to set records that no man had ever equaled. He was fated to take part in 466 races and rallies, win 194 times and place in the first four 307 times.

But now it was 1955, fairly early in his career, and he was about to tackle Italy's famous Mille Miglia—and he was demonstrating to the racing fraternity what it takes in dedication and alertness to win what experienced drivers called the toughest race in the world. . . .

The race was scheduled for April 30, 1955, but Moss and his co-driver, Denis Jenkinson, were at the Mille Miglia circuit early in February—almost three months before race day. There was a reason. The two drivers were going to chart the entire 1,000 miles of the circuit!

Stirling Moss had been consistently overshadowed by the great Juan Manuel Fangio in Grand Prix competition. Fangio was slated to start in the Mille Miglia too, and Moss was anxious to gain revenge for several defeats he had suffered at the hands of the fine Argentinian driver. Moss was driving for Mercedes Benz that year, and he was grimly determined to beat Fangio in the toughest race of all.

"There's only one way to win the Mille Miglia," Moss told his co-driver Jenkinson. "That is to learn the thousand-mile route so thoroughly that we can post a faster average than any other driver."

It was an ingenious plan but a far from simple one. Unlike other races, the cars did not begin the race from a starting grid but left Brescia at one-minute intervals. The driver who completed the thousand-mile marathon in the shortest time was the winner. Most drivers, realizing the magnitude of trying to memorize the entire thousand miles, contented themselves with learning the toughest sections only.

"We're going to learn the entire course," said Moss. "Every curve and hill and dip in the road!"

It was a large order, but Moss and Jenkinson proceeded to tackle the problem. While Moss drove, Jenkinson sat beside him and made notes on a roll of paper. He would chart every curve, making an appraisal of its sharpness and the maximum speed at which it could be taken. He would mark down all the straights, indicating how long they were and what speeds could be reached on them. He counted every hill, and whether or not the top of the hill hid a sharp curve or a straightahead road. He charted bumpy stretches, bridges, towns, roadside markers, everything.

"The idea is this," explained Moss, "if we're climbing a hill and we know there is a curve just beyond the crest of the hill, then we know we have to slow down. However, if we know that the road continues straight, we can hit the hill at top speed. Other drivers, not remembering if there is a curve on the other side of the hill, will brake. We'll gain seconds by not braking."

It was a good idea, but there was one important thing about it—they had to be right. If they miscalcuated and hit a hill at top speed thinking a straight road lay ahead, and if instead there was a sharp curve, it could mean a wreck and possibly their deaths.

Moss and Jenkinson circled the Mille Miglia roadway an endless number of times, and when they had finally charted the entire course they had a roll of paper almost twenty feet long. With the roll of information, Jenkinson was to be the navigator and keep driver Moss continuously aware of what was coming next.

But how to communicate? The noise of the Mercedes Benz engine precluded conversation. So instead Moss and Jenkinson devised a system of hand signals and memorized them.

The race started at 9 P.M. on April 30, but it was not until after 7 A.M. the next morning that Moss and Jenkinson took off. The reason? There were more than six hundred cars in the race!

As soon as the Mercedes Benz was on the road the plan went into action. Moss got the car up to 170 miles per hour, and Jenkinson signaled him in advance as they swept into curves and climbed hills. Other drivers, less certain about what lay behind the crests of hills, braked—

Campari and Ramponi winning the Mille Miglia in 1928 in an Alfa Rome 1500.

but not Moss. Moss streaked along, hitting the tops of hills so fast that at moments he was airborne, relying implicitly on the signals being sent him by Jenkinson.

Moss had complete faith in Jenkinson—a necessary ingredient if the plan was to work at all. When Jenkinson signaled that a straight road lay behind a hill over which Moss could not see, Moss tramped down on the accelerator instead of the brake. Faith, at 170 miles an hour, is some faith indeed! For at such a speed, there is no margin for error!

The twisting road led from Brescia, through Verona, toward Padova. At this point Moss noticed a Ferrari gaining on him and, dismayed at the way the Ferrari driver was cutting the distance between them, Moss sped into Padova at about 150 miles an hour. Jenkinson signaled frantically that there was a sharp right-angle turn ahead, and Moss responded by trying to brake his speed in time. He managed to do it, but his tail fished on him and struck one of the straw bales along the road. It slowed him up just enough to permit the Ferrari to streak past him.

Moss was a cagey driver, and he noticed at once that the driver of the Ferrari was pushing his car like a madman. Moss knew that if he stayed on the tail of the Ferrari, and something happened in front of him, it might be curtains. So he wisely lagged a little, waiting for the Ferrari driver to push his car beyond its endurance.

Already, scattered along the road, were the hulks of other cars that had, for one reason or another, quit the race. And then the thing that Moss anticipated happened. The Ferrari, driven furiously, began to weave. The next moment the driver pulled off the road and into the pits at Ravenna—about the 200-mile mark in the race. Its tires were almost bald, and as the pit crew worked on it, Moss passed.

Following the Apennines through Rimini and along the Adriatic coast, Moss pushed his own car to the utmost. The car responded like a thing alive. One after another Moss passed slower-moving cars that had started the race ahead of him. And at many curves he saw the wrecks of cars that had gone off the road or come to rest with noses mashed against a tree. When Moss and Jenkinson were finally forced to stop for gas at Pescara, they received the news that they were in second place, only fifteen seconds behind the leader.

After Pescara the road led into the mountains, turning and bending as it climbed the heights. Moss drove like the master he was, taking every curve at the maximum permissible speed, but no faster.

Five hours after leaving Brescia the Moss-Jenkinson team was in Rome, where they had to make a sixty-second stop to refuel and have the rear wheels changed. Then they were off again on the return lap to Brescia.

They were now in the lead, with the second-place car a full two minutes behind them!

There is an old saying about the Mille Miglia that "he who leads at Rome never leads at Brescia," and this proverb went through Moss's mind as he gunned the car along at a 150-mile-an-hour pace. Well, maybe they could defeat the odds that said the leader in Rome must eventually lose.

Moss drove with the precision of a physician operating on a patient. Jenkinson handed him signals as an intern or nurse hands the physician scalpels and bandages. And the physician at the wheel of the Mercedes Benz accepted them without question.

And then Jenkinson missed a signal!

The only reason it happened was that Jenkinson suddenly felt a spray on his face and turned his head instinctively. In that split second Moss approached a dangerous right-hand turn, hidden by the crest of a hill. Moss became aware of it just in time and braked down, skidding around the curve. Jenkinson, embarrassed, stole a glance at Moss, who was cornering with one hand, shaking his fist in anger at Jenkinson with the other and telling him off in words Jenkinson could not hear—and preferred not to.

There was another dangerous moment a little later on. This time Jenkinson signaled a left-hand turn, but Moss took it too fast. The Mercedes Benz spun out and slid, back-end first, into a shallow ditch. But Moss was worthy of the challenge. With the second-place car gaining on him, he shifted into first, pulled out of the ditch, fishtailed onto the road and sped away with a challenging roar from the exhausts to frighten off any close pursuer.

The Italian sun was pitilessly hot, but it seemed not to bother Stirling Moss. Jenkinson was aware, if Moss was not, that the great English driver was outdoing himself. He was almost perfection at the wheel, for after more than 700 miles of high-speed driving he still retained all his skills and all his alertness.

At Florence the Mercedes Benz bounced over rough streets and grade crossings at 125 miles an hour. Then it was across the Arno River, and into the Apennines again toward Bologna.

Moss did not know what was happening behind him, whether someone was whittling down his lead time or not. And so he drove fast and without letup.

Then, quite suddenly, it was over—and Stirling Moss was the winner, posting an average of 97.93 miles an hour and turning in the 1,000 miles in 10 hours, 7 minutes and 48 seconds. His old nemesis, Juan Manuel Fangio, was second in another Mercedes Benz—but he was more than half an hour behind.

Moss basked in the glow of victory and then, finally, relaxed after his long drive. But a few hours after completing the grueling 1,000-mile Mille Miglia, Moss turned to Jenkinson and said, "I think I'll leave for Germany tonight."

"Tonight?" Jenkinson's eyes popped. "How will you go?"

"Oh," said Moss easily, "I'll drive."

THE TARGA FLORIO 3

Achille Varzi

The Targa Florio, held on the island of Sicily, just off the toe of Italy's "boot," is the oldest surviving road race in the world. The first Targa Florio was run in 1906 and, with only a few exceptions during World War I and World War II, has been held every year since.

The course itself has changed. In 1906 the long Madonie Circuit was used, a twisting road that skirted the entire circumference of the island. Today the course has been shortened (it is called the short Madonie), but one facet of it remains the same. It is a course laid out through savage mountains that reach an altitude of 3,700 feet—a winding, climbing, then descending road that offers a supreme test to both men and machines.

The Targa Florio is named after Count Vincenzo Florio, a Sicilian who was an avid racing fan back in the very earliest days of the sport. In 1904 he offered a cup for a race in Brescia, Italy, and shortly thereafter announced that he would promote the Targa Florio on his home island. It turned out to be quite a race indeed.

It was May 6, 1906, and ten cars were lined up at the starting point near Palermo to engage in the race. As the time came for the dropping of the flag, the monster cars roared and chugged and puffed like dragons, and mechanics swarmed over the behemoths in a frantic attempt to keep the engines going. The cars were crude by today's standards. Most were four-cylinder jobs, huge, unwieldy and with few refinements. But they would run—at least for a time—and that was all that was asked of them in those days. Among the cars were such names as Fiat, Clement-Bayard, Mors, Itala, Berliet and Hotchkiss.

The statistics of the race are now history, but intimate details are meager. The course was 90 miles long, and for much of the time the cars were in the mountains out of sight of onlookers. There were breakdowns—one Itala lurched to a stop in the mountains when it lost its fuel, a Clement-Bayard hit a boulder and broke its axle, a Fiat lost compression on two of its cylinders, a Hotchkiss had multiple tire trouble.

Even the winner had difficulties, but luckily it didn't occur until he had crossed the finish line. Alessandro Cagno, driving an Itala, charged across the finish line with a 29.07-mile-per-hour average for the 277.3 miles of the course—and went into such a frenzy of happiness that he jammed down on the brakes so hard he stripped the crown wheel. He could not have traveled another ten feet, but he didn't have to. He had won the race.

The Targa Florio today is run over a circuit about half the distance of the older races. But because of the terrain over which the racers must run, it is the slowest major race in the world. Average speeds have increased only about thirty miles since Cagno won the first race at 29.07 miles an hour. But despite slower speeds, it is one of the most rugged of the races that count in the sports car manufacturer's world championship.

Over such a course, you can expect that many memorable races have been run. One of the most keenly contested races was the 1930 Targa Florio, which merits special mention.

If you've studied your history you will know that in the year 1930 the Fascist dictator Benito Mussolini was in power. Like all dictators, he was determined to prove that Italy was superior to other nations in all things. This included the manufacture and racing of automobiles.

French Bugattis had won the Targa Florio for five years in a row—and this was a point of great humiliation to the Italians. It was being said that Il Duce "would not permit" another Italian defeat—that he "demanded" that an Italian car driven by an Italian driver win in 1930.

Politics and national prestige had, as we've seen in other races, raised their ugly heads—and, in so doing, promised one of the most fiercely fought Targas of all time. The car on which Italian hopes rested was the Alfa Romeo, and one of the men in the Italian team on which Italian hopes depended was Achille Varzi. . . .

Achille Varzi was born on August 8, 1904, at Galliate in the province of Novara, Italy. From very early days he was interested in racing of all kinds. Like the other great Italian driver of the time, Tazio Nuvolari, he started as a motorcycle racer in the 1920s. Later he began to drive on four wheels instead of two, and from that time on a great rivalry existed between the two finest Italian drivers of the day—Varzi and Nuvolari.

Varzi became known as a stylist in racing circles. Driving was an art to him. He had an uncanny ability to evaluate not only the circuit on which he planned to race, but the cars of his opponents and his own car. Before he ever entered a race, Varzi would calculate how the race would logically be run—and this edge in thinking often gave him the tiny advantage he needed to win. He was

Felice Nazzaro in a Fiat, winner of the Targa Florio in 1907.

a consistent driver, able to get the most out of his car under any given set of circumstances; and although he was not as flamboyant or dramatic as many, he was considered to have "class"—which about summed up the feeling that knowledgeable racing men had for him.

In 1929 Varzi purchased his own car—an Alfa Romeo —and entered his first major race. It was the European Grand Prix at Monza. He finished second to Louis Chiron, who drove a Bugatti, but he opened the eyes of racing fans all over the world with his impeccable performance. That same year he finished third in the difficult Mille Miglia, first in the Rome Grand Prix and again first in the Monza Grand Prix—and he missed the title of Italian Champion by a fraction.

Now it was 1930 and he was in Sicily, and on this little Latin man with the unnaturally blond hair rested the honor of all Italy, not to mention the peace of mind of Benito Mussolini. . . .

Achille Varzi's big two-liter Alfa Romeo was not exactly built for the tricky Madonie Circuit. Many men wise in the ways of racing thought Varzi was being handicapped by driving the car, for it would take a man of unparalleled skill to handle the Alfa Romeo over the hills and curves presented by the Targa Florio course. But from the outset Varzi proved himself to be just the man to manage the problem. He drove with a skill and talent that earned the respect of the men who understood racing best. In fact, Varzi got away to a tremendous start by finishing the first circuit in 1 hour, 21 minutes and $21\frac{3}{5}$ seconds, to set a lap record for the Targa Florio.

But it turned out, as everyone expected, to be the most hotly contested Targa Florio of all time. Varzi was not the only driver to break the existing lap record. Two other Italian drivers also broke it. So did three of the detested French Bugattis. It was a race with everything at stake, and the drivers were pushing their cars to the utmost limit.

With his first fast lap to start him off, Varzi led in the race most of the way, but he was continually pressed by other racers that hung on grimly, just far enough behind to take immediate advantage of any mistakes he might make.

Then, with two laps to go, Varzi ran into difficulty.

At one point of the mountain circuit, spring rains had washed out the road. The repairs to the route before the race had been hurried, with the result that there was a frightfully rough spot where the drivers had difficulty even keeping their fast-moving cars on the road. It was at this point that Varzi's spare tire, set in the tail of his car, was jarred lose. It dangled for a moment, rubbing the gas tank until a hole formed, and then it fell off the car.

Now the chips were really down. Louis Chiron, the French champion, driving a hated Bugatti, was gaining ground on Varzi. Varzi knew he would have to make a stop for gasoline, now that his tank was punctured and leaking, whereas the Bugatti had already been refueled for its last time and could now finish the race without a stop. That could well eat up the slight 31-second lead Varzi had. Not only that, but he would now be forced to finish the last two laps without a spare tire—and if he should suffer a puncture it would be the end of everything.

Varzi slammed into the pits, was refueled and rushed out again—at a discouraging cost in time. Now he was thirty seconds *behind* the Bugatti. He pressed down hard on his accelerator—a desperate driver, now, a half-minute behind his chief rival, and driving a car with no spare tire and a leaking gas tank!

If a blowout or puncture didn't stop him, then there was a strong possibility that he would run out of gas before he made it to the finish line!

At the refueling station Varzi's riding mechanic had grabbed an extra can of gas, intending to refuel the car as it ran, if necessary. On the last lap, with gas getting low, the mechanic took the can and attempted to pour gas into the tank as Varzi continued to travel at an almost crazed speed.

The attempt was disastrous. The speed of the car and the roughness of the road made a careful filling of the tank impossible and some of the gasoline spilled over the tail of the racer and hit the redhot exhaust pipe.

Flames licked up over the car, reaching out toward Varzi and the mechanic!

"We're on fire!" screamed the mechanic.

Varzi felt the heat of the flames on his neck, but he did not panic. He hunched forward in his seat and drove like a madman.

"We're too close to the finish to quit now," he said grimly.

The mechanic fought the flames with a seat cushion, attempting to smother them, and Varzi gamely continued his nightmarish drive as if nothing was happening.

Finally the mechanic succeeded in smothering the flames. Varzi raced through the last town on the circuit, Campofelice, and hit the five-mile straight that ran along the Tyrennian Sea. It was the longest straight of the course, and Varzi was relying on the speed of the big Alfa Romeo to win for him at this point. He jammed the accelerator to the floorboards and never let up.

The car would either win for him or blow up. There was no alternative.

The car held up, and Varzi whipped past the grandstand the victor in the twenty-first Targa Florio. He had won the race by a margin of slightly over one minute.

An Italian driver in an Italian car had won for Italy, and Dictator Benito Mussolini slept well that night.

THE TWELVE HOURS OF SEBRING 4

Mario Andretti, Bruce McLaren

The little town of Sebring, Florida—halfway between Miami and Ocala—is an unlikely place for an important automobile race. While most of the European road racing circuits are scenic and hilly, the Sebring course is flat and uninteresting. But since Sebring's twelve-hour sports car race is always held in the latter part of March, there are plenty of tourists on the Florida peninsula to serve as spectators. Not only that, but the race has gained sufficient stature to attract American race fans wherever it might be held.

The first race over the pretzel-shaped 5.2 miles course at Sebring was held in 1950 and was of six hours' duration. The race was doubled to twelve hours in 1952, and finally gained status as a world championship sports car event in 1954. In 1959 the United States Grand Prix for Formula 1 cars was held at Sebring, but in 1960 it was moved to Riverside, California, and later to Watkins Glen, New York. But for this one exception, Sebring has been, and is, the sports car racing center of the United States.

In the first sports car championship race of 1954, a Cadillac-Allard won the honors with an average speed of 66.59 miles an hour over a six-hour run. The race was not a glowing success from the standpoint of the number of spectators present, nor did the event pick up much more attention in 1955. It was not until 1956 that the Sebring race gained stature, when the great Juan Manuel Fangio made his first appearance and won.

Early in the 1960s the red Ferraris from Italy began to dominate the race, which had become the Sebring Twelve Hours of Endurance Race. But on the horizon was an American car-maker with a strong desire to challenge and eventually defeat the foreign cars which were grabbing the honors in the world's top sports car races. This car-maker, as we have seen, was the Ford Motor Company.

By 1966 Ford was ready to make its move—with two major driving teams ensconced in Ford Mark IIs: Lloyd Ruby and Ken Miles, and Dan Gurney and Jerry Grant. There was also a Holman-Moody Ford and a Ford GT 40 entered in the race—a race that was fated to become one of the wildest, and most tragic, ever held at Sebring.

Sebring patterns the start of its Twelve Hours of Endurance Race after Le Mans, where the drivers race on foot to their cars and whip them into squealing, snarling action. At exactly 10 A.M. the Governor of Florida dropped the green flag and the drivers sprinted for their cars. Gurney's car was at the head of the line at the start, thanks to a qualifying lap of two minutes and fifty-four seconds, and it was apparently Ford strategy to let Gurney lead the pack. But Gurney had an unexpected one-minute bout with a balky Ford and, when it finally did start, he took

Alfa Romeo, Inc.

Alfa Romeo "33" coupe in its American debut at the 1967 Sebring.

after the pack of leaders like a wolf on the trail of a deer.

Dan Gurney had a tough time catching up. Mike Parkes in a Ferrari was leading the parade and setting a brisk pace. For over an hour Gurney pursued him. Finally, on the twenty-eighth lap, Gurney moved into the lead—but immediately the lead was jeopardized by the fact that he was forced to make two quick pit stops to the Ferrari's one.

A driver named Bob Bondurant took over the Ferrari on its pit stop, and when Gurney roared away from his second stop he held only a three-second lead over the stubborn Ferrari.

Gurney set a blistering pace in his Ford Mark II and inexorably stretched his lead over the Ferrari. But no sooner had he disposed of one pest than another appeared. The second major Ford driving team—Ken Miles and Lloyd Ruby—had passed the faltering Ferrari and was now contending with Gurney for the lead.

Miles was in the second Ford, and he had no intention of conceding the race to Gurney. On the thirty-eighth lap the two drivers dueled wheel to wheel, bringing the crowd to its feet with excitement.

At about this time the race was marred by a terrible tragedy. A Ford GT 40, driven by Bob McLean, left the road on a tight hairpin turn. It all happened in a flash— the car became airborne, struck a pole and exploded. The shattered wreckage flipped end over end several times, came to a rest upside down and flames consumed it immediately.

McLean was killed in the fiery crash.

But the race went on. At 7 P.M.—just three hours from the finish—the Gurney-Grant team still led, but not by much. Right behind was the Ruby-Miles car.

At 8 P.M. it was the same.

Then, at 8:30, another accident occurred. Mario Andretti, a rookie driver who was to make a name for himself in racing, brought his Ferrari into the pits. But as he did so the rear wheels of the car locked and Andretti went into a slide. The car hit a retaining wall, bounced back on the track, and collided violently with a Porsche Carrera.

Ford Motor Company

Ford GT at Sebring.

The Porsche went off the track, struck four spectators who were in an unauthorized area and crashed into the concrete supports of a fuel oil tank. The Porsche driver suffered only a broken ankle and shock, but all four spectators were killed.

This tragic event—the second of the race—gave all the advantage to the Fords on the track. Both Andretti's Ferrari and the Porsche were out of the race, and now the lineup looked like this: Gurney-Grant, in the Ford Mark II, first; Ruby-Miles, in a Ford Mark II, second; Hansgen-Donohue, in the Holman-Moody Ford, third; Scott-Revson, in the Ford GT 40, fourth.

It was 9:55, with only five minutes to go in the race, when Hard Luck Gurney experienced one of his typical misfortunes. A timing chain broke on his Ford Mark II, and the stricken car coasted to a stop on the final turn before beginning the last lap. A stunned and surprised Ken Miles, in the second Mark II, roared past and took the checkered flag. He and his co-driver, Ruby, had traveled 228 laps at an average speed of nearly 99 miles an hour, eclipsing the previous record of 92.4.

The Holman-Moody Ford was second and the Ford GT 40 third. Ford had defeated the foreign cars with a vengeance, grabbing first, second and third places in one of the most tragic races in Sebring history.

The following year, 1967, Ford was back at Sebring again, determined to add to its luster in the field of racing. This time they had a stellar team in their Ford Mark IV Sports prototype—Mario Andretti, the up-and-coming new driver and two-time winner of the United States Auto Club (USAC) Championship, and Bruce McLaren, a veteran driver who had captured the Twenty-Four Hours of Le Mans the year before. . . .

Mario Andretti was born in 1940 near Trieste, Italy. His young life was periled by World War II, and when Trieste was partitioned he spent three years in a displaced persons camp. Despite his difficulties, he had time to worship personal heroes, as boys always do. Mario's hero was Alberto Ascari, the Italian World Champion Driver.

When he moved to America in 1955 and took lodging

with relatives in Nazareth, Pennsylvania, he received his
first opportunity to own and race cars. A natural, he did
very well in any type of car—Indy-type racers, stock cars
and sports cars. To open the 1967 season he drove a Fair-
lane stock car into the winner's circle at NASCAR's biggest race, the Daytona 500.

Bruce McLaren was a native of New Zealand and
started his racing career in 1953. After five years he had
established himself as one of the top drivers "down under." In 1958 he left for the European racing scene, and
in 1959 he made connections with the Cooper team and
posted his first major Formula 1 victory in the United
States Grand Prix at Watkins Glen, New York. In 1966
he had teamed with fellow New Zealander Chris Amon
to drive a Ford Mark II-A to victory in the Twenty-Four
Hours of Le Mans.

Now both of these exceptional young drivers were
together as a team in the Twelve Hours of Sebring. . . .

April 1, 1967, was not a typical Florida day. Dark,
threatening clouds hung over the track, and there was a
wind of fifteen miles an hour that occasionally rose to
gusts of thirty—enough to give drivers in the big race an
extra problem.

The consensus of opinion was that the Fords—the
Andretti-McLaren Ford Mark IV and the A. J. Foyt-Lloyd
Ruby Ford Mark II—were fast enough to win the race
and could ride to victory *if* their brakes held out. The
twisting, turning Sebring course required unusual use of
the braking system, and those who resented the intrusion
of American cars on the scene took refuge in the feeling
that the Ford braking system was not up to par.

As it turned out, the chief fly in the Ford ointment
was the Chaparral driven by Jim Hall and Mike Spence.
This weird-looking car with pronounced wings set the
pace most of the afternoon, and for hours was engaged
with the Andretti-McLaren Ford in wheel-to-wheel racing.

For a long time it was nip and tuck. The Andretti-
McLaren Ford grabbed the lead early in the race, but the
Chaparral was always on its tail. During the second hour
of the race, with Andretti at the wheel, the Ford Mark IV

Ford Motor Company

The Ford Mark IV made its debut, driven by Mario Andretti and Bruce McLaren in the 1967 Sebring Race.

posted an amazing lap of 109.090—a record for the Sebring circuit. But following this spectacular performance, Andretti had to pull into the pits for gas and oil. He was there two minutes—enough to give Spence in the winged Chaparral an opportunity to grab the lead.

Andretti raced out of the pits and took the lead back, only to lose it again to the Chaparral on lap 57 when he had to take the Ford back into the pits again. That's the way it went most of the afternoon, with first one and then the other of the two cars leading.

The other cars in the race were presenting no serious challenge to the two leaders. A Porsche and a Ferrari collided, and both were eliminated from the race. Another Ferrari quit with gearshift trouble. A Corvette also disappeared from the scene with mechanical difficulties.

Andretti and McLaren drove with extreme determination all afternoon, because it was obvious that the Chaparral was a fast car that was quite capable of winning the race—except for one thing. The Chaparral drank gasoline in frightful gulps, and as a result had to return to the pits more often than the Ford Mark IV.

But when it was on the track it was a real speedster. Three times the Chaparral broke track records, first posting a speed of 110.377 miles an hour, a few laps later raising it to 110.769 miles an hour, and around four o'clock in the afternoon zooming around the track at 111.032 miles an hour.

And then, suddenly, at 6:11 P.M., the Chaparral went out of the race. All at once it was engulfed in a cloud of smoke and oil sprayed from a blown differential. At 7 P.M., following the withdrawal of the Chaparral, the rundown was announced: the Andretti-McLaren Ford Mark IV was first, the Foyt-Ruby Ford Mark II was second and a German Porsche was holding third.

That's the way they finished. The Fords were one-two —Andretti-McLaren completing 198 laps, and Foyt-Ruby second with 197 laps. The Porsche, third, had 188 laps.

The Fords, in two consecutive races, had served notice on the racing world that they were a power to contend with for many years to come.

PART FOUR

OVAL TRACK RACING

THE INDIANAPOLIS 500   1

Ray Harroun, Bill Vukovich, Jim Clark

Europe early in the century embarked on a road racing program which was ultimately to realize its greatest potential in Grand Prix competition. In America, however, racing took a completely different direction. Except for the brief interval of the Vanderbilt Cup road races, which were canceled because of the danger to spectators, Americans seemed to prefer to race on oval tracks.

In the early days of the automobile, these tracks were exceedingly primitive. They were dirt tracks, often full of ruts and holes, muddy when the weather worsened and tough on the inadequate tires of the day. There were a lot of them scattered around the country, and the automobile was enough of a novelty in those days to lure spectators to the races in fairly large numbers.

One of the most important races of the century's first decade occurred in Grosse Pointe, a fashionable suburb of Detroit. It was important because it made two men— a race driver and a manufacturer—prominent figures in the automotive world.

One was Barney Oldfield, the other was Henry Ford.

The year was 1902. Alexander Winton, a Cleveland car-maker, was recognized as the racing champion of the United States. He drove a formidable car called the Bullet, and none of the other American manufacturers—Duryea, Haynes, Olds, Maxwell, Stanley, White or Franklin— could beat him.

Henry Ford was an upstart to this elite list of manufacturers, but he was a young man determined to build a car that would beat anyone—Alexander Winton included.

With his partner, bicycle racer Tom Cooper, Ford built two racing machines—the "999" and the Arrow. The "999" seemed to be the better of the two cars, and Ford decided to race it against Winton and his famed Bullet. There was only one problem—finding a driver.

Neither Ford nor Cooper cared to drive the monster they had created in a race. The big, ugly car had four huge cylinders that produced eighty horsepower and drove the car forward at a speed unheard of at the time. Finally they decided to engage the services of a daredevil named Barney Oldfield—a bicycle racer who had never driven a car in his life!

On October 25, 1902, the big race began under rainy skies and a slightly moist track. Lined up against Oldfield and the "999" was Winton in his Bullet, a man named Buckman in a Geneva Steamer, Shanks in a vehicle called the Pup and White in a White Steamer. All the bets were on Alexander Winton to win the race with ease.

But Oldfield had different ideas. He got away to a surprising start, leaving the Bullet behind. Alexander

Ford Motor Company

An interesting shot of one of the races at the Indianapolis 500.

Winton was so startled that it took him a lap or two to regain his composure. Then he began to close the gap on Oldfield and the "999."

But Oldfield proved himself to be a spectacular driver. He drove with complete recklessness, taking the curves just as fast as he took the straights—a practice that was not recommended if you wanted to stay alive. The pace proved too much for the famous Bullet; it coughed, sputtered and finally withdrew from the race.

Oldfield won the short, five-mile race with a time of 5:28. As a result of his victory two things occurred. Oldfield was launched on a racing career that was to make him an American legend, and Henry Ford was given the impetus to start him on his career as an automobile industrialist.

Other dirt-track races were held in various parts of the United States in the early years of the twentieth century. As the popularity of the sport grew it was inevitable that racing enthusiasts would eventually attempt to upgrade the events. Finally four men got together and decided it was time to create an oval track of higher quality with permanent grandstands where spectators could be shielded from harm by high-flying automobiles.

The result was the Indianapolis Speedway.

The four men primarily responsible for its creation were Carl G. Fischer, James A. Allison, A. C. Newby and Frank H. Wheeler. All of them were businessmen, and all of them had vision. They arranged to purchase 328 acres of flat land only a few miles from downtown Indianapolis, and on it they built a 2½-mile oval track. Heavy expenses made it impossible for them to pave the oval at once, and the four ringleaders had to settle for a track of crushed limestone and gravel.

The first race held on the new track was not an automobile race at all. It was a motorcycle race. The day turned out to be heavy on dust and light on thrills, and promoters of the event correctly decided that the customers had already had their fill of motorcycles.

On August 19, 1909, the first auto race was held at the big new speedway. It was billed as a three-day auto-

mobile "carnival of speed"—and that it was. Barney Oldfield—the cigar-chewing, rambunctious race driver who
some authorities now claim was more of a showman than
a skilled driver—was the big name in the race. He kept
his name big by winning the first day's 250-mile event
in a Blitzen Benz that turned up a new world's record of
43.1 seconds for a mile, or 83.4 miles an hour.

But tragedy accompanied the spectacular win. The
wheels of the racing cars stirred up clouds of dust, and
two drivers, blinded by the impenetrable screen, were
killed.

On the second day of the carnival Louis Strang, in
a Buick, won a 100-mile race, and this one was free of
accidents.

The third day was a real wingding. There were two
races scheduled. The first featured a grinding duel between Barney Oldfield and another famous name in racing, Ralph de Palma. Oldfield's Blitzen Benz managed to
finish a scant 150 yards ahead of de Palma's Fiat.

The second race was a 300-mile affair, and the
furious friction of sixteen cars on the track's limestone
and gravel base was too much for it. Dust swirled again,
and one of the cars crashed through a fence. Although
the driver escaped injury, the mechanic was killed, along
with two spectators.

That was too much. The race was stopped and the
crowd sent home. An aura of gloom settled over the
promoters of the track. Five people had been killed in
three days of racing. There were only two alternatives—
either pave the track at great expense or close it up and
admit failure. The promoters decided to pave it.

The track was resurfaced with brick, from which it
got its early name, The Brickyard.

On Memorial Day, May 30, 1911, the first 500-mile
race was held. Some 80,000 people showed up. Each had
his favorite driver—big names of their time like Johnny
Aitken, Ralph de Palma, Louis Strang, David Bruce-
Brown, Howdy Wilcox, Art Chevrolet, Ralph Mulford
and Spencer Wishart.

And back in the sixth row of the starting pack was

a lesser-known young man named Ray Harroun, driving a six-cylinder Marmon Wasp—*with a rear-view mirror!*

There was a story behind that rear-view mirror. It was customary in those days for each race car to carry a driver and a mechanic. Harroun, however, had decided to drive the 500-mile grind alone. When other drivers realized this they began to protest.

"Without a mechanic in the seat next to you, you're a menace on the track," they said.

"How so?" Harroun wanted to know.

"Without a mechanic to tell you when cars are coming up from behind to pass you, you constitute a hazard on the track," they said. "We may decide to lodge an official protest and have you barred from the race."

"All right," said Harroun. "Tell you what I'll do. I'll put a mirror on the cowl of my car so I can see cars approaching from the rear."

This unheard-of arrangement confounded the protesters, and they dropped their charge. Harroun then rigged up a mirror on the cowl of his Marmon Wasp. It was the first rear-view mirror ever used on an automobile!

Forty cars were entered in the race, and when all of the engines were started at once the roar almost deafened those in the grandstand. Then the flag was dropped and the closely packed cars moved forward, following the pace car for the first lap.

The cars made the circle, came back in front of the grandstand and roared loudly and threateningly as the pace car glided into the pits. The first 500-mile race was on!

Aitken and de Palma set the pace at first, only to be overtaken by a driver named Fred Belcher who had never driven in anything more competitive than a hill climb.

The lead changed among several drivers as the laps were ticked off; but no one at this point was going into gleeful hysterics over the performance of Ray Harroun. He was well back in the pack, and with forty laps already gone it looked as if he would stay there.

Then a rash of mishaps occurred. One racer blew a tire, then another, followed by several more. As one car

Barney Oldfield in the old "999" racer, Henry Ford standing.

after another limped into the pits, Harroun found himself moving up in the race—without even increasing his speed!

At sixty laps (150 miles) Harroun held second position. He kept his car moving at a steady 75 miles an hour, refusing to be panicked into a greater speed to pass the leader or to fend off those behind. His strategy was to drive at a speed he knew the Marmon Wasp could handle, and wait for the other cars to fall apart.

In general, this plan seemed to be working, but eventually it was Harroun who had to bring the Marmon Wasp into the pits for a tire change. When he stopped, Cyrus Patschke, a relief driver for Harroun, jumped behind the wheel. By the time the tire was put on, the Marmon Wasp was in fifth place.

David Bruce-Brown was now in the lead, with the Marmon Wasp a full minute behind. Patschke managed to slice four seconds off this lead, but could do no better.

"I'll take over," said Harroun, and the pit crew flagged Patschke in.

Patschke came in after completing the 102nd lap, an equivalent of 255 miles.

Harroun got a break the moment he pulled out of the pits. Bruce-Brown was in for a tire change. Harroun gunned it around the oval and grabbed first place before Bruce-Brown could get back on the track. Now he led Bruce-Brown by a full lap.

At this point the pace began to tell. Car after car went out of the race with mechanical trouble. Some of that trouble caused oil to slick the brick track. The going became hazardous, but Harroun continued to average his 75 miles an hour.

But now he was being pressed. Most of the cars had fallen well behind or were out of the race entirely. But Ralph Mulford, in a Lozier, began to gain on Harroun. Harroun kept watching him in his rear-view mirror. He was sure that Mulford would require a tire change shortly, and if so, that would be the break Harroun needed to win.

Then, to Harroun's amazement, his own right rear

tire burst! The Marmon Wasp swerved agonizingly, and Harroun fought the wheel. Mulford roared ahead of him as he reluctantly pulled into the pits.

But Mulford's lead lasted only until he, too, was forced into the pits for a tire change. That put Harroun ahead again with 140 miles to go.

Mulford's Lozier ripped out of the pits with determination, and in his rear-view mirror Harroun saw the big car gaining on him again. Before he knew it the Lozier was alongside him, wheel to wheel. For minutes the two racers kept abreast, and then the Lozier took the lead.

There were now only 24 laps to go!

That looked like the finish for Harroun and the Marmon Wasp. Harroun trailed along behind the Lozier, but still Harroun refused to panic. He stubbornly kept his 75-mile-an-hour speed, making no effort to pass the speeding Lozier.

The strategy paid off. Mulford's Lozier finally failed under the relentless pressure, sputtered in a dying gasp and pulled over to the side. Harroun sped past the stricken car and took the checkered flag after six hours and 42 minutes of driving.

The steadiness of the race Harroun had run was reflected in his average speed for the entire 500 miles—a cool 74.59 miles an hour.

Ray Harroun went down in racing history as the first man to win the Indianapolis 500!

That was the beginning, and since that time almost every famous race driver in this country—as well as many from other countries—has taken part in the Indianapolis 500. Famous names, dating from the opening of the track through the 1920s, include Ray Harroun, Ralph de Palma, Barney Oldfield, Tommy Milton, Peter DePaolo and Wilbur Shaw. The 1930s and 1940s saw more famous racers emerge, among them Louis Meyer, Wild Bill Cummings, Mauri Rose, Floyd Roberts, Chet Miller, Rex Mays and Duke Nalon. The 1950s and 1960s have boasted their stars too, and these names may be the most familiar to you: Johnny Parsons, Tony Bettenhausen, Troy Ruttman, Jim

Rathmann, Bill Vukovich, Fred Agabashian, Rodger Ward, A. J. Foyt, Dan Gurney, Lloyd Ruby, Jack Brabham, Mario Andretti and Bobby Marshman. There were many others, too numerous to name, who belong on any complete role of outstanding drivers.

Of all these famous drivers, I have selected to tell the story of Bill Vukovich. My reason is that, of all the drivers in the last two decades, Vukovich is one who seems certain of immortality in the minds of racing fans. Bill Vukovich had amazing stamina, raw courage and a toughness of character that made him one of the most spectacular drivers ever seen on the Indianapolis Speedway. He drove a race car with a boldness and dash that amazed his opponents, and because of his derring-do behind the wheel of a car he earned the nickname of The Mad Russian. . . .

Bill Vukovich was born in 1919 in Alameda, California. Two years later his family moved to a farming community outside Fresno, California, where young Bill was raised. He had two brothers, Eli, fourteen, and Mike, eighteen. There were also five girls in the famliy.

When Bill was thirteen years old his father died, and this made it necessary for the boys in the family to go to work. Bill, Eli and Mike picked cotton, worked in orchards, drove trucks and did odd jobs whenever they could be found.

In 1937 young Bill, always fascinated by cars, persuaded a friend to let him drive a souped-up Chevrolet in a stock car race. In 1938 he arranged to drive in a midget auto race, and in his first midget race cracked three ribs and his collarbone in a crash. His brother Eli also became a race driver. The two of them traveled from one midget track to another, and often each brother would drive twenty races a day.

During World War II racing came to a stop, and young Vukovich went to work repairing jeeps and trucks. He bought himself a midget car, and as soon as racing was resumed in 1945 he was back on the tracks. He won race after race, always driving with a recklessness that dismayed his opponents. He crashed fairly often and was injured a lot, but he always bounced back to race again. In

Ford Motor Company

A. J. Foyt in the 1968 Indianapolis 500.

1946 and 1947 he was West Coast Midget Champion, and in 1950 he was National Midget Champion—and then, rather abruptly, interest in midget racing dwindled, tracks began to close and Vukovich decided to try the big cars.

In 1951 Vukovich qualified a car called the Central Excavating Special at Indianapolis and found himself in the famous 500 for the first time. He didn't expect to win.

"This crate will go thirty laps and fall apart," he predicted.

It went twenty-nine, sprung an oil leak and was out of the race. But the twenty-nine laps had provided Vukie, as he was becoming known, with racing experience on the big oval.

Vukovich was back for the 1952 race with another car—and might have won had not the car failed him. He was out front with only eight laps to go when his steering wheel broke and he came to rest against a retaining wall. Disgusted but unhurt, he climbed up on the wall and watched the finish of the race. During the time he was watching the other drivers, he made a decision.

"I'll win it next year," he said to himself. "It's a cinch. All you have to do is keep turning left."

That was the simple racing philosophy with which he entered the 1953 race. . . .

Memorial Day, 1953, was a stifling hot day in the 90s. Vukovich drove a Keck Fuel Injection Special—and how he drove it! The temperature was so intense that one driver died of heat exhaustion, and only five drivers drove the entire 500 miles without relief. Vukie was one of them. And he won.

In 1954 he repeated, posting a record-breaking speed of 130.84 miles an hour.

With two consecutive wins at Indianapolis under his belt, Vukovich was a young man much in demand. He was asked to drive in the Pan-American Road Race and eagerly accepted. He almost drove his co-driver out of his mind by the reckless manner in which he took curves.

"Slow down on the curves," the co-driver warned, "or you'll end up against a tree."

Vukovich said nothing, continuing to drive like the "Mad Russian" he had become.

"Take it easy, Vukie!" yelled the co-driver again.

Vukovich paid no heed.

"You want to put us over a cliff?" screamed his partner.

Vukie did not answer

Finally the thing the co-driver dreaded took place. Vukie missed a curve and the car sailed over a 30-foot drop-off. As the car was airborne, Vukovich took his hands off the wheel.

"Okay, fellah," he said. "*You* drive it."

Fortunately, neither man was hurt.

When the time came for another Indianapolis 500 in 1955, Vukovich had a new car capable of close to 180 miles an hour. Vukie entered the race with his usual determination to win. Nobody had ever won three Indianapolis 500s in a row, but that didn't faze Vukie. He decided he would be the first.

Almost 200,000 spectators were on hand to witness the big race. A total of thirty-three cars started, and the speeds were phenomenal. Cars slammed around the track at speeds up to 175 miles an hour, and Vukovich drove with his usual skill and daring. At the end of thirty-five laps he was in the lead, and he was coming up behind the last-place car, having lapped the field.

Then something went wrong in front of him. One of the speeding cars caromed off the wall and bounced back on the track. A second car avoided hitting the stalled automobile, but struck a third car. For precious seconds the entire track was blocked—and Vukovich, traveling at better than 150 miles an hour, had time neither to swerve nor to apply brakes.

Vukie hit one of the cars broadside, and his own car leaped high in the air. It landed nose down, then bounced end over end seven times. By the time the ambulance reached the scene, Vukovich was dead. He had died of a fractured skull, seconds before the car broke into flames and burned up.

The saga of Bill Vukovich, one of the most remembered race drivers of all time, was ended.

It is difficult to select any Indianapolis race and rate it above others. But upsets are always interesting, probably because American fans love to see an underdog win in any athletic endeavor. That's why we must mention the first Indianapolis 500 to be run after World War II—on Memorial Day, 1946.

At this particular time the king of American race drivers was a man named Ralph Hepburn. He was entering his fourteenth race at Indy, which gave him an edge over the field in down-to-earth experience. Moreover, he had set a qualifying record for the race with an average speed of 133.944 miles an hour. All around him were other top drivers—Tony Bettenhausen, Rex Mays, Sam Hanks, Duke Nalon, Paul Russo, Mauri Rose and Cliff Berger.

And then there was George Robson.

Virtually no one knew George Robson. He was one of quite a few in the thirty-three-car lineup who wasn't given a chance to complete the race, much less win it. He sat in the fifth row of the starting grid, in a Thorne Engineering Special—a somewhat doubtful car owned by one Joe Thorne of Hollywood, California.

The official pace car led the racers around the track for one lap, then pulled off into the pits. Motors revved and the race was on, the cars heading for the first turn like a pack of hound dogs on the scent. The thirty-two-year-old Robson was in the middle of that pack, unnoticed by the 180,000 spectators viewing the race. After all there were Hepburn, Mays, Bettenhausen, Rose, Russo and Nalon to watch—and if anybody at all mentioned George Robson the reply would have been "George *who*?"

And possibly no one would have known about George Robson after the race either had it not been for a lot of strange and unaccountable happenings on the track that afternoon.

Suddenly, as the cars roared along in a nice even rhythm, chaos began to emerge. Incredible and unbelievable things began to happen, like Paul Russo slamming his car against the retaining wall and leaving the race, like Rex Mays going into the pits at the sixtieth mile with a broken manifold, like Tony Bettenhausen going out with a faulty connecting rod, like Duke Nalon being eliminated by a broken differential, like Cliff Berger's car developing oil leaks after two hundred miles and like the favorite, Ralph Hepburn, failing to finish because of a broken connecting rod!

One by one, all the top drivers were being forced off the track with mechanical difficulties!

Cars were falling apart all over the place, in a rash of failures never before seen at the track—and taking the places of the top drivers as pace-setters were three lesser-known drivers, one of them George Robson!

The other two were a stranger named Jimmy Jackson and a one-time winner, Ted Horn.

"Horn and a couple of kids up front," scoffed one official. "At least Horn has been around before, so you have to figure he will win it. Those kids haven't got the savvy to blow him off the track."

Still at the 350-mile mark, Robson and Jackson were battling it out in front, wheel to wheel, while Horn lay back in third place. The wise heads figured that Horn would wait for the proper moment and then burn his way past the two green leaders.

But it didn't work that way. Horn never really challenged the two front-runners. And little by little, Robson drew ahead of Jackson. When the 500-mile grind was completed, it was George Robson, the man nobody knew, who took the checkered flag.

He had beaten a veritable bevy of top drivers against whom he had been given no chance!

One oddity of the race was that only four cars out of the thirty-three starters finished. Wilbur Shaw, president of the Indianapolis Speedway at the time, blamed the rash of car failures on the fact that parts for cars were in limited supply following the end of World War II, but he said it did not detract from Robson's fine finish.

"You have to admit, his car lasted," he said. "And so did he."

One of the finest drivers to come upon the racing scene in more recent years was the late Jim Clark. As a driver, this indomitable Scotsman was close to perfection.

His philosophy of racing was to determine the absolute safe speed on both straights and curves and then systematically stay within those limits. This approach to racing required great courage as well as unparalleled skill, and Jim Clark had both.

Born and raised in the lowlands of Scotland, Clark was fascinated by speed from boyhood. His efforts in speed started with his legs and ended with automobiles. In school he was a sprinter. Later he raced bikes. Finally he raced cars.

When he was twenty years old he entered his first automobile race—the only one that year. At twenty-one he raced twice. But he made his first real splash in the racing picture in 1958 when he joined a group of racing enthusiasts called the Border Raiders. Their technique was to drive into England, enter a race or two, pick up some money, and carry it back to the Bonnie Land of the Heather.

Jim Clark's father was not happy about his son's penchant for racing. The elder Clark was a farmer, raising crops, sheep and cattle. He owned two farms in Scotland and had put young Jim in charge of one of them. But racing began to take up a lot of Jim's time, and as a result he had to neglect duties around the farm. This nettled his father at first but Clark eventually made his name and fortune in racing and his father grew proud of his achievements.

Probably Jim Clark's greatest contribution to racing was on the Grand Prix circuit, but Americans will remember him best for what he accomplished at Indianapolis. Clark came to the big oval Speedway in 1963. This was the year that would see him emerge as the World Champion Grand Prix Driver, but the hardened veterans of "The Brickyard" were not impressed with his record in road racing. Oval-track racing, they claimed, was different— and anybody who came out of European road racing with the idea that he could win the Indy had to be out of his mind.

In Clark's case, the Indianapolis crowd was even more contemptuous. This quiet, easygoing Scotsman had a strange car powered by a Ford engine—and that was good for a lot of laughs in Gasoline Alley. Everybody knew that it took an Offenhauser-powered car to win the Indianapolis 500, and to expect a Ford engine to hold up under the prodding of a stranger to oval-track racing was expecting too much.

But both Clark and the Ford engine surprised the experts. The engine held up and so did Clark, finishing only 34 seconds behind winner Parnelli Jones in the long, grueling grind.

That opened a lot of eyes in racing circles, and when Clark returned to Indy in 1964 he was treated with a little more respect. But he had bad luck that year: a tire blew when he was leading the pack, and he went out of the race early.

A few of his opponents started to breathe easier immediately thereafter. Then came 1965.

Clark, who had become the World Champion Driver in 1963, was well on his way to capturing the same title in 1965. When he showed up at Indianapolis in his Lotus-Ford, nobody laughed or even chuckled. They knew, now, that Clark was a man—perhaps *the* man—to beat. The Offenhauser-powered cars had a formidable challenger in the Lotus-Ford.

Clark by this time was known as the "Flying Scot," and he took off on a typical flying start when the flag dropped for the 1965 Indianapolis Classic. He was leading the pack when he swept into the first turn, and he led it most of the way thereafter. Only once, on the second and third laps, was he challenged, and Clark overcame the threat easily. On the second lap A. J. Foyt forged ahead of him, but Clark got the lead back on the third lap. He led in 190 of the 200 laps and won the race with comparative ease—the first foreigner to win at Indy since 1916, the first to win in a rear-engine car and the first to win with a Ford engine. And he set a track record besides—his average speed being 150.686 miles an hour, over three miles an hour faster than the preceding record.

A lot of oval-track devotees were slow to admit it, but they finally were forced to acknowledge that both

Jim Clark and Ford-powered racers would have to be reckoned with for some time to come. For in addition to Clark's victory, other Ford-powered cars did extremely well. In fact, Ford-powered cars took the first four places! Clark won in his Lotus-Ford, Parnelli Jones was second in another Lotus-Ford, rookie driver Mario Andretti took third in a Dean Van Lines Ford and the fourth spot went to Al Miller in an Alderman Ford.

In April, 1968, tragedy struck. Jim Clark, considered by then the greatest race driver of all time, was killed in a terrible crash at Hockenheim, Germany, when his Lotus-Ford-Cosworth left a straightaway, somersaulted several times and smashed into a tree. He died instantly of a compound skull fracture and a broken neck.

PART FIVE

THE STOCKS, THE MIDGETS AND OTHER THINGS

STOCK CARS AND MIDGETS 1

So far in this book I've covered what might be called the "elite events" of motor racing—Grand Prix competition, major sports car races and the Indianapolis 500. Now let's examine other forms of racing and rallying that have become popular all over the country in recent years.

Stock car racing—now an exciting and important sport in America—actually developed hand-in-hand with the motorcar in this country. Early automobile manufacturers not only had to produce cars but were required to convince the American public that automobiles were here to stay. The best way to gain recognition for their products was to race them—just as European car-makers were doing. So stock car racing got under way somewhere around the turn of the century.

By the time of World War I (1914–18) cars were pretty much accepted by the American public. Perhaps it was that acceptance, as well as the fact that many Americans were just getting interested in driving and tinkering around with their own cars, that cast stock car racing into the doldrums after the war ended. But following World War II, strangely enough, interest in stock car racing revived.

In 1947 the National Association for Stock Car Auto Racing (NASCAR) was formed by Bill France and William R. Tuthill of Daytona Beach, Florida. The association was an immediate success and has grown in power and prestige over the years.

Each year NASCAR promotes a racing program at Daytona Beach that has become one of the major events in stock car racing in this country. Today there is a fine speedway where this annual event is run, but in earlier days the race was run partially over the hard beach sands near Daytona. It was one of the strangest racetracks in the world. Route A1A, down the east coast of Florida, constituted one of the straightaways. The other straight was the hard sand of the beach when the tide was out. The curves connecting the two straights at each end were banked with sand. It was the only track in the world where an overeager or careless driver could get stuck in the sand on the curves or blow a tire on the beach and end up in the Atlantic Ocean.

A rival promoter to NASCAR is the United States Auto Club (USAC), which promotes major races all across the country. Between them, they sponsor many races. NASCAR races include: 500-mile races at Riverside, California; Daytona, Florida; Atlanta, Georgia; Rockingham, North Carolina; Darlington, South Carolina; Charlotte, North Carolina; 400-mile events at Daytona and Darlington; and a 600-mile affair at Charlotte.

Ford Motor Company

Stock Car racing, David Pearson in the lead.

Ford Motor Company

The Blitzen-Benz in 1911 at Daytona, Fla.

Races by USAC include: two 200-mile races, two 150-mile affairs and a 250-mile race at Milwaukee, Wisconsin; a 300-mile and a 150-mile race at Indianapolis, Indiana; a 300-mile race at Riverside, California; and races in Montreal and Quebec City.

Stock car racing is particularly popular in the southern states. Drivers become well known, and although many stay in stock car racing during their entire careers, there have been quite a few who have gone on to Indianapolis or into Grand Prix competition.

Testifying to the popularity of stock car racing in this country, nearly 53,000,000 fans watched the contests in 1967.

In the 1940s another type of racing flourished for a while. This was midget car racing. At the time there were many racing enthusiasts who simply couldn't afford the kind of big cars needed for major races, such as the Indianapolis 500. These people decided to build small, less expensive cars—and the result was midget racing. Almost anything was used for an engine in these little bugs—old and obsolete car engines, motorboat engines, motorcycle engines. These were installed in lightweight little bodies and pepped up with special fuel. The cars were capable of a top speed of perhaps 85 miles an hour.

Races were first held on dirt tracks. Later, as the midget craze gained in popularity, special tracks were built. For a time midget races drew large and enthusiastic crowds; but the spell finally wore off, and midget racing is rarely heard of today.

THE SPORTS CAR PHENOMENON 2

In another section of this book I covered the top sports car races of our time. These races are entered only by the top drivers of our time—the professionals who make racing their entire life. The sports car, however, is a popular automobile to many people who would never consider getting bchind the wheel and racing at Le Mans or Sebring. These are the car enthusiasts—you and I—who own a sports car and are in love with it, and who have a desire to use it in some form of competition where they can demonstrate its superiority over others.

The result of this desire has been a variety of sports car events, such as economy runs, rallies, gymkhanas, trials and hillclimbs. All of these events are different, all of them are thrilling to the car enthusiast and all of them draw sizable crowds.

One of the most popular forms of sports car competition is the rally. Contrary to what the uninitiated might think, this is not a race. It is, in fact, an exacting time-and-distance test that taxes both the driver and his passenger (called a navigator) to the utmost.

It works this way. A route is laid out over which the cars will travel, and a predetermined average speed (always lower than the legal limits on the roads to be used) is set. Cars are released from a starting point at about one-minute intervals, and each car is required to complete the route as close to the predetermined average speed as possible. In other words, if an average speed of 35 miles an hour is set for the course, the car is required to travel as close to that speed as possible over the entire route. It does no driver any good to exceed the speed limit set, for the winner is not judged on his speed; the car that comes closest to the average predetermined speed is always the winner.

In such a contest the navigator is as important as the driver—and in many respects more important. He is the one who uses stopwatches, precision mileage counters and other devices to keep the driver at the average speed. So skilled have drivers and navigators become at keeping their car right on the button that the winner is often determined by a matter of seconds. Two or three seconds late—or early—over the course can mean loss of the rally to the erring driver.

Occasionally the rally promoter will decide to add extra hazards to the competition. This is accomplished by adding "gimmicks" to the race—scrambling street names, codes that have to be deciphered to determine the exact route and other devices. But the straight time-and-distance competition is the most popular type and provides for the proud owner of a sports car a means of competition that is both exciting and safe.

The gymkhana is another popular type of sports car competition. This is an event that tests not only the skill of the driver but the maneuverability of the car. Gymkhanas are usually held on a huge parking area—often on Sundays, when normal parking is limited. The parking lot is set up with special lines and pylons, which create an obstacle course for the drivers and cars. Cars are required to slalom—as in skiing—around pylons; drivers may have to back up into a tight spot made up of pylons; sometimes they will be required to hit a certain speed and then stop suddenly within a designated area. Winners are judged on the skill with which they accomplish the task of maneuvering the obstacles set in their path.

Sports car trials are similar to gymkhanas in the sense that car and driver are required to overcome certain obstacles, but the obstacles are usually natural ones—hills, creeks, mudholes, rutted fields, etc. Both driver and car must be in top condition to survive this kind of test— and after such a contest many cars can be seen stuck hub-deep in mud, stalled on hills and even sitting ducklike in the middle of streams.

Many people—both participants and spectators—enjoy an event known as the hillclimb. This is a race against time—uphill. Cars are started off one at a time at the bottom of a steep and difficult hill. The object is to get to the top of the hill in the least elapsed time. Curves and steep grades make this a thrilling exhibition.

Another competitive event is the economy run. This contest is strictly what its name implies—an attempt on the part of the driver to accomplish a certain distance in the most economical fashion. There are two ways to work this. Sometimes a certain distance is prescribed, and cars are given exactly the same amount of gasoline; the car reaching the finish line with the most fuel left is the winner. Another way is to fill the cars with the same amount of gasoline and drive them until they run out of gas. The driver covering the greatest distance by the time he runs out of gas is the winner.

The economy run is not only a test of skillful and careful driving, but also a test of the driver's mechanical ability. Owners of the competing cars exhibit considerable genius in preparing their cars for a mileage test. They may use lighter oil or special lubricants, inflate their tires to make them roll with greater ease and tinker endlessly with their engines to get the last ounce of power out of the last ounce of gasoline.

In addition to all these events, there is also the "minor league" of sports car racing. Sports car fans who never expect to race at Le Mans or Sebring nevertheless do race on other circuits in this country. These circuits are usually made up of privately owned roads that are used to simulate the kind of European roads over which the great sports car races are held. Most of the races are supervised by the Sports Car Club of America (SCCA), and regulations are similar to those of the big races. To take part in these events, however, you must qualify for a competition license.

THE LURE OF THE DRAG STRIP 3

One of the fastest-growing American sports today is drag
racing. Those who love cars and thrill to their performance, but who never expect to race professionally for the
big money, are participants in the sport. The amazing
thing about drag racing is the fact that, on any given
Sunday, you will find approximately 3,000,000 fans lining
the drag strips of the nation to watch these roaring exer-
cises in acceleration.

That, as a matter of fact, is what drag racing is all

Two contenders in the 1956 National Championship Drag Races at Kansas City, the nicely constructed Mercury engined dragster, left, and the powerful airplane engined "Green Monster."

about—not a race in the true sense of the word, but a contest to see who can go "from here to there" in the fastest burst of acceleration.

There was a time when drag racing was considered a dangerous pastime. This reputation came about when irresponsible young boys participated in drag racing on open roads, where other cars and drivers were endangered. Today drag racing is carefully supervised on drag strips created for the purpose.

To the individual who enters his car in competition, drag racing is an extension to owning a car. These owners are proud of their cars and the performance they can coax out of them, and they enjoy competing against others with similar pride in their automobiles. It has a unique appeal to the spectator too, since many of the cars he sees in action on the drag strips are the same kind that he drives to work every day. And if you own, say, a Mustang or a Corvette, it gives you a moment of pride to see *your* car win on the drag strip.

There are three categories of drag racing: dry lake bed racing over courses three to five miles long; the all-out attempts to set world land speed records over the 14-mile-long Bonneville salt flats of Utah; and drag racing over the quarter-mile strip. It's the last of these with which we will concern ourselves, since it is by far the largest participant-spectator category of all.

There are approximately sixty classes of competition in drag racing today. In order to equalize competition, each class has carefully defined limits imposed on weight, engine power and other factors. In quarter-mile runs, the equality of the cars puts a premium on the driver's skill: the winning time usually goes to the driver who handles his car best.

Most of the cars appearing on the nation's drag strips are regular production cars. They are called "factory cars" and are the same kind of cars you see on the road every day. However, even among these factory cars there are some forty classes of drag racing.

In another class are the "altered" cars. Rules for altering a production automobile are many and strict, but in

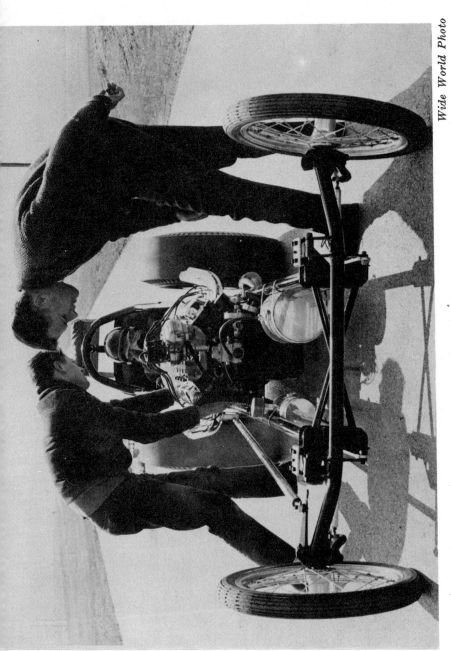

Don Gunther in the cockpit of the specially designed dragster he built with the help of his brothers,

general the altered class permits restricted hopping-up of the engine and mild reduction in weight of chassis and body.

A modified class permits more general tinkering with the engine power of the car. The car can be stripped until it is extremely light, and the engine can be shifted to the rear, if desired, to provide greater rearward traction.

The ultimate in performance, however, is reached in the dragster class. These vehicles are weird-looking contraptions that often weigh less than 1,200 pounds and boast engines up to 1,300 horsepower. They will roar down a quarter-mile track at speeds in excess of 200 miles an hour. The dragster is often called a rail, rail job or fueler, and there are virtually no restrictions on what you can do to make this monster perform.

Drag racing is the sport of the people who love cars more than anything else in the world.

POSTSCRIPT

The complete story of automobile racing—including every race of every type from that first one in 1894 to the present date—would take many volumes. Indeed, telling such a comprehensive story might be an impossibility. In this book I have attempted to tell the history of auto racing in condensed form, citing only some of the most memorable or significant races. But there is enough here to show you that auto racing is a thrilling—and many times, danger-ous—sport, and you are probably by now asking yourself that key question that has been asked so many times by so many people.

Why do men race?

Men race because, instinctively, man is a combative creature. This combative nature, this craving for competition, is evident in almost all of man's endeavors. There is peaceful competition in the business world, in the arts and in the sciences. There is nonpeaceful competition in war.

Between these two extremes is a wide gap, and to satisfy his combative and competitive nature man has created sports to fill it. Baseball, football, basketball, hockey and other sports help to satisfy man's unquenchable thirst for team combat. Individual combat—one man against another—occurs in boxing, wrestling, fencing and other hand-to-hand engagements. Isolated combat—man against nature—is seen in fishing, hunting and other outdoor sports.

Racing probably falls in the individual-combat bracket, for usually it is one man against another. And racing is as old, perhaps, as any sport known to man, for it has existed, in some form or another, almost from the beginning of man's life on earth.

Obviously, the first form of racing was on foot. But man quickly showed a genius for racing not only himself but anything that moved. Animals, particularly, have been used by men for purposes of racing. Men have raced horses, both with a rider up and a rider in a cab behind (chariot and harness racing). In Egypt, men race camels, and in many countries, dogs. And, strange as it seems, men have even raced turtles and—yes—beetles.

It's not surprising, then, that when a form of "horseless carriage" was invented, men began to race these too.

There is an old story about a mountain climber who was standing at the foot of Mount Everest and looking up at the top wistfully.

"Why do you want to climb it?" asked a friend.

The mountain climber shrugged. "I guess, just because it's there," he answered simply.

This anecdote, which illustrates man's will to conquer, fits automobile racers as well. They want to race cars because they are there. The sleek car, with its powerful engine capable of driving it at unbelievable speeds, is a challenge to the kind of men who race. They must take that car out and see how fast it will go. They must test it against other cars to see which is the best. They must perfect their individual driving skills so that they can win —at least most of the time.

The combative nature of man—the desire to win, to beat someone else, to come out on top in a titanic struggle —is all there when men get behind the wheel of a fast automobile.

Someday, in some distant future, automobiles will be looked on as quaint vehicles of an ancient time. By that time man will have at his disposal other more refined means of transportation, such as wheelless vehicles that glide just above the ground on a cushion of air. Eventually, he will be racing to the moon in space ships.

But today—in our time—automobile racing is the ultimate in the use of speed on land. Men will continue to race, and thousands will watch them, until something better replaces the sport that many say is the greatest of them all.

INDEX

Agabashian, Fred, 186
Aitken, Johnny, 181, 182
Alcyon, 76
Alfa Romeo, 57, 59, 63, 64, 95, 116, 125, 159, 161, 163
Allison, James A., 180
Andretti, Mario, 168, 170–171, 173, 186, 195
Arcangeli, Luigi, 116
Arrol Johnston, 76
Arrow, 178
Ascari, Alberto, 71, 77, 78, 80, 85, 95, 118, 119, 120, 122, 125, 137, 170

Aston-Martin, 106, 110, 134, 137, 139
Atlanta 500, 145
Austin-Healy, 134, 143, 150
Automobile Club of France, 42, 49, 71
Auto racing,
early French, 12–15, 17–23; early American, 18, 53–56; town to town, 17–23; long distance endurance, 25–40; International, 41–51; accidents, 20–23, 85, 116, 143, 146, 168–169, 189, 195; drivers, 57–65, 70,

Auto racing (*cont.*)
71, 77–81, 85–88, 94–95, 110,
124–125, 136–137, 144–145,
150–151, 159, 170, 171, 185,
186, 192; Grand Prix, 69–129,
133, 134, 144, 175, 192, 197,
205; sports car circuit, 133–
173; oval track, 175–195;
stock car, 197–205; midget,
186, 188, 205; drag strip, 211–
215; reasons for, 217–219

Behra, Jean, 88, 89, 98
Belcher, Fred, 182
Belgian Grand Prix, 109–114,
145
Bennett, James Gordon, 41, 42,
44, 49
Benz, 74
Berger, Cliff, 190, 191
Bering Straits, 34
Berliet, 158
Berlin, 30, 34
Bettenhausen, Tony, 185, 190
Blitzen Benz, 181
B. M. W., 150
Boillot, George, 76
Bondurant, Bob, 168
Bonneville salt flats, 213
Donnier, Joakim, 105–107
Bordeaux (France), 17, 20, 21,
23
Bordini, Pietro, 116
Borghese, Prince Scipione, 27,
28, 30
Borzacchini, Mario, 116
Brabham, Jack, 71, 87, 105, 106,
107, 186
Brassier, 71, 74
British Grand Prix, 104, 123–129
British Racing Motors (BRM),
104, 109
Brivio, Antonio, 57, 64, 65
Brooks, Tony, 91, 98, 109, 110
Bruce-Brown, David, 181, 184
Bugatti, 65, 85, 159, 161, 162
Buick, 181

Cadillac-Allard, 166
Cagno, Alessandro, 158, 159
Calthorpe, 76
Campari, Giuseppe, 116
Caracciola, Rudi, 70

Central Excavating Special, 186
Chaparral, 171, 173
Charron, Ferdinand, 42
Chasseloup-Laubat, 19
Chatellerault, 22
Chevrolet, 94, 186
Chevrolet, Art, 181
Chicago, 18
Chicago Times Herald, 18
Chiron, Louis, 70, 85, 161, 162
Clark, Jim, 71, 191 192, 193,
195
Clement, Albert, 55, 56
Clement-Bayard, 54, 55, 56, 71,
74, 158
Colignon, M., 27, 29
Collins, Peter, 95, 97, 98, 99, 100,
112
Cormier, M., 27, 29
Connaught, 77, 110
Contal, 27, 29
Cooper, Tom, 178
Cooper, 77, 88, 105, 106, 107, 109,
150
Cooper-Climax, 87, 88, 89, 91
Corvette, 144, 213
Cote, 76
Coupe International, *see*,
Gordon Bennett Races, first
race
Cummings, Wild Bill, 63, 185
Czaykowski, Graf, 116

Darracq, 71
Daytona Beach, 200
Daytona 500, 145, 171
De-Dietrich, 54
De Dion Bouton, 11, 12, 13, 14,
18, 27, 29, 30, 34, 37
Denzel, 144
DePaolo, Peter, 185
Dion, Marquis de, 11, 12, 13, 14
Drag strip racing, *see*,
auto racing, drag strip
Driver's World Championship,
70
Duryea, J. Frank, 18
Dutch Grand Prix, *see*,
Grand Prix of Holland

Economy run, the, 209, 210
Edge, S. F., 44, 45, 47–49, 51
Excelsior, 76

Fangio, Juan Manuel, 71, 77, 78, 80–81, 93–101, 118, 119, 120, 122, 124, 125, 127, 137, 151, 156, 166
Farina, Giuseppe, 57, 71, 85, 95, 118, 119, 120, 122
Federation Internationale de l' Automobile (FIA), 70, 112
Ferrari, 57, 77, 112, 118, 119, 120, 122, 125, 128, 129, 134, 137, 139, 144, 145, 146, 147, 154, 166, 168
Ferrari, Enzo, 144
Fiat, 54, 55, 71, 73, 76, 116, 158
Fischer, Carl G., 180
Florio, Count Vincenzo, 158
Ford, 94, 134, 144, 145, 146–147, 166, 168, 170, 171, 173, 193, 195; Mark IV, 144, 147, 170, 171, 173; Mark II, 166, 168, 170, 171; Mark IIA, 171; GT 40, 166, 168, 170; "999," 178, 180; Lotus, 193, 195
Ford, Henry, 178, 180
Foyt, A. J., 144, 145, 146, 147, 171, 173, 186, 193
France, Bill, 200
French Grand Prix, 49, 69, 70, 71–81, 124, 129

Gabriel, M., 23, 73
Geneva Steamer, 178
German Grand Prix, 59, 61, 93–101
Giaccone, Enrico, 116
Gobi Desert, 26, 28, 29
Gobron-Brillie, 71
Godard, Mynheer, 27
Gonzalez, Froilan, 77, 78, 124, 125, 127, 128, 129
Gordinis, 77
Gordon Bennett Races, 25, 44, 49, 53; first race (1900), 42–43; Irish race (1903), 49, 51
Grand Prix, see, auto racing, Grand Prix
Grand Prix of Holland, 103–107
Grand Prix racers, see, racing cars, Grand Prix
Grand Tourismo (GT), see, sports cars
Grant, Jerry, 165, 170
Gregoire, 71, 76

Gregory, Masten, 105, 106, 107
Grosse Pointe, 178
Gurney, Dan, 144, 145, 146, 147, 166, 168, 170, 186
Gymkhana, 208, 209

Hall, Jim, 171
Hanks, Sam, 190
Harroun, Ray, 182, 184, 185
Hawthorn, Mike, 71, 77–81, 95, 97, 98, 99, 100, 101, 112, 113, 114, 118, 120, 125, 127, 143
Hepburn, Ralph, 190, 191
Hill, Graham, 71
Hill, Phil, 71
Hillclimb, the, 209
Horn, Ted, 191
Hotchkiss, 71, 158
Hourgières, G., 19
Hulme, Dennis, 71
H. W. M., 77

Indianapolis 500, 63, 144, 145, 150, 181–195, 197, 205
Indianapolis Speedway, 180, 181, 186
International Grand Prix, 88
Itala, 27, 28, 29, 30, 158
Italian Grand Prix, 115–122

Jackson, Jimmy, 190
Jaguar, 134, 137, 143
Jenatzy, Camille, 42, 51
Jenkinson, Denis, 151, 152, 154, 155, 156
Jones, Parnelli, 193, 195

Keck Fuel Injection Special, 188
Knyff, René de, 42, 51

Lancia, 134, 144
Lancia-Ferrari, 95
Lautenschlager, Christian, 74
Le Mans (France), 71, 110, 134, 136, 137–143, 144, 145–147, 166, 170, 171, 207
Levassor, Emile, 18
Levegh, Pierre, 136, 137–143
Liège (Belgium), 30
Lion-Peugeot, 76
Long Island, 53, 54, 63
Lorraine-Dietrich, 71, 73, 74, 76

Lotus, see,
    Ford, Lotus
Lozier, 184, 185
Lytle, Herbert, 56

McLaren, Bruce, 171, 173
McLean, Bob, 168
Macklin, Lance, 143
Madonie Circuit, 157, 158, 161
Marimon, Onofre, 118, 119
Marmon Wasp, 182, 184, 185
Marshman, Bobby, 186
Maserati, 77, 78, 93, 95, 97, 118,
    119, 120, 122, 128, 129, 144
Materassi, Emilio, 116
Mathis, 76
Mays, Rex, 185, 190
Mercedes, 51, 54, 55, 71, 74, 76,
    116
Mercedes-Benz, 95, 123, 124, 125,
    128, 137, 139, 141, 143, 151,
    152, 155, 156
Meyer, Louis, 145, 185
MG, 134
MG Magnette, 61
Midget racing, see,
    auto racing, midget
Miles, Ken, 166, 168, 170
Mille Miglia, 59, 61, 77, 95, 134,
    149–156, 161
Miller, Al, 195
Miller, Chet, 185
Milton, Tommy, 185
Monaco, 83, 88
Monaco Grand Prix, 59, 61, 70,
    83–91
Mongolia, 26, 28
Monte Carlo, 83, 84
Monza (Italy), 59, 60, 115, 116,
    134
Monza Grand Prix, 59, 60
Morgan, 150
Mors, 23, 51, 74, 158
Moscow, 26, 30, 34
Moss, Stirling, 77, 88, 89, 98, 106,
    110, 112, 114, 118, 125, 127,
    128, 129, 137, 150–156
Moto-Bloc, 34, 37, 74
Mulford, Ralph, 181, 184, 185
Musso, Luigi, 98
Mussolini, Benito, 159, 161,
    163
Mustang, 213

Oldfield, Barney, 178, 180, 181,
    185
Opel, 74
Oval track racing, see,
    auto racing, oval track
Owens, Percy, 51

Packard, 54
Palma, Ralph de, 181, 182,
    185
Panhard, 13, 18, 19, 42, 49, 51,
    54, 55
Panhard-Levassor, 71, 74, 94
Paris-Amsterdam race (1898),
    19
Paris-Berlin race (1901), 19
Paris-Bordeaux race (1895),
    17–18, 26
Paris-Dieppe race (1897), 19
Paris-Lyon race (1900), 42
Paris-Madrid race (1903), 20–
    23, 25, 41
Paris Matin, 26, 30, 31, 33
Paris-Rouen race (1894), 12–
    15, 26
Paris-Troubille race (1897), 18–
    19
Paris-Vienna race (1902), 19,
    44–49
Parkes, Mike, 168
Parsons, Johnny, 185
Patschke, Cyrus, 184
Peerless, 51
Peking to Paris race (1907),
    26–31
Peugeot, 12, 14, 18, 76
Pons, Augustin, 27, 29
Pope Toledo, 54, 55, 56
Porsche, 134, 144, 168, 169, 173
Porthes, 74
Protos, 34, 37, 40
Pup, the, 178

Racing cars,
    French, 12–15, 19, 42, 55, 74;
    early engineering of, 20; Brit-
    ish, 104–107; German, 71, 74,
    76, 123, 124, 125, 129; Ameri-
    can, 42, 178; Grand Prix, 133,
    134
Rally, the, 208
Ranier, Prince, 84
Rathman, Jim, 186

Renault, 54, 55, 71, 73, 74
Renault, Louis, 23
Rheims circuit, 76
Riverside (California), 144, 166, 205
Roberts, Floyd, 185
Robson, George, 190, 191
Rolland-Pillain, 76
Roosevelt Raceway, 57, 63
Rose, Mauri, 63, 64, 145, 185, 190
Rouen (France), 12, 13, 14
Royal Tourist, 54, 55
Ruby, Lloyd, 165, 168, 170, 171, 173, 186
Russo, Paul, 190
Ruttman, Troy, 185

San Francisco, 34, 37
Schell, Harry, 98, 105
Sebring circuit, 134, 145, 165–170, 171–173, 207
Shaw, Wilbur, 63, 64, 145, 185, 191
Siberia, 26, 29, 34, 37
Singer, 76
Sivocci, Ugo, 116
Sizaire-Naudin, 34, 76
S & M Simplex, 54
Spence, Mike, 171, 173
Sports cars, 133, 134, 207–215; circuit races, 133–173
Sports Car Club of America (SCCA), 210
Spyker, 27, 29, 30
Stapp, Babe, 63
Stock car racing, see, auto racing, stock car
Strang, Louis, 181
Sunbeam, 76
Surtees, John, 71
Szisz, M., 73

Talbot, 137, 139
Targa Florio, 134, 157–163
Thomas Flyer, 34, 37, 40
Thorne Engineering Special, 190
Tourist Trophy Race, 61
Triumph, 134
Troubille, 18
Tuthill, William R., 200

Udde (Mongolia), 28, 29
United States Auto Club (USAC), 200

Valdez (Alaska), 34
Vanderbilt Cup Races, 25, 53–57, 61–65, 175
Vanderbilt, George, 56
Vanderbilt, William K, 53, 54, 56
Vanwall, 106, 109, 112, 113, 114
Varzi, Achille, 61, 70, 159–163
Vauxhall, 76
Versailles, 18, 20
Villoresi, Luigi, 78, 80, 95, 118, 120, 137
Vinot-Deguignand, 76
Vukovich, Bill, 186–189
Vulpes, 71

Ward, Roger, 186
Wheeler, Frank H., 180
White Steamer, 178
Williams, W. G., 85
Wimille, Jean Pierre, 65
Winn, Billy, 63
Winton, Alexander, 42, 178, 180
Winton Bullet, 51, 178, 180
Wishart, Spencer, 181

Zborowski, Count, 116
Zandvoort, 103
Zust, 34, 37, 40